PRAISE FOR WHY WE LOVE BACK TO THE FUTURE

"*Why We Love Back to the Future* by Brad Gilmore is one of the most engaging flights of fancy you will have. Gilmore has given us unique stories and ideas you will love for all time. Be an Earth Angel and give this some time to marinate in your brain. It's sure to set you on a new time travel adventure."

—**Harry Waters, Jr., actor (Marvin Berry)**

"Brad Gilmore has managed to take a magnifying glass to a classic movie series we're all familiar with and find new, interesting ways to look at why fans around the world connect with it. His love for the franchise is bolstered by depth, insight, and a warm reverence for the films. Great Scott, this is a must-read."

—**Ken Napzok, author of *Why We Love Star Wars***

"I can't think of a more qualified aficionado of all things *Back to the Future* to write a book celebrating its popularity with fans around the world."

—**Jeffrey Weissman, actor (George McFly in Parts II and III)**

"Brad Gilmore proves you don't have to be an '80s baby to be obsessed with this trilogy. His enthusiasm feels just as fresh as when the movies were released. I'm pretty sure he owns shoes with automatic laces at this point. He knows so much about BTTF, you'd swear he was in the passenger seat of the DeLorean the whole time. So strap in, because when this baby hits eighty-eight mph you're going to see some serious shit."

—**Jenn Sterger, radio and TV host**

"Brad Gilmore is the constant professional. He brings energy and enthusiasm to everything he works on. And nothing can be truer than his passion and love for *Back to the Future*. I want to read this book and I'll even buy a copy (although I should get one for free)."

—Kristian Harloff, host of *The Kristian Harloff Show*

"*Back to the Future* has been one of my favorite movies since I first saw it in movie theaters. Brad does a good job of bringing back the feelings of what made the movies so special to me and the entire world. Now can you dig that!"

—Booker T, two-time WWE Hall of Famer

"As film franchises go, no one has done more for the dynamics of time travel than *Back to the Future*. And no one has poured themselves into the mythology, humor, and gravity of the films like Brad Gilmore. If there was a religion of Doc Brown, Brad would be the chief pastor able to teach you everything."

—Brandon Caldwell, journalist

"Brad seamlessly straddles the line between *Back to the Future* superfan and expert, which makes him both the most entertaining and informative source on the subject matter around. His book is as accessible to *Back to the Future* die-hards as it is to new fans."

—Kyle Hubbard, critically acclaimed musician

"Equal parts critical exploration and celebratory toast, Brad Gilmore's book not only offers new perspectives and a deeper understanding of *Back to the Future*, it reminds us why we fell in love with it in the first place."

—Mark Ellis, comedian and movie critic

"I remember being very ignorant to the *Back to the Future* series my entire life; I hadn't seen many movies growing up and honestly I wasn't very interested until I was introduced to this film by Brad Gilmore's perspective and I was completely sold on the film(s) and had to watch. Immediately after digesting his review, I watched the movie and I experienced it in a way I couldn't have without the exposure to his love for the film. I couldn't tell if I had been sold on something and was jumping on the bandwagon or if I genuinely had become a fan, but either way, I was engulfed. Brad has a way of making things within life feel larger than life and that's exactly what he did for me, this film, and this book. Ever since, I've bought into anything he's told me about, and he hasn't let me down yet."

—Stockz, major recording artist

"Brad's enthusiasm and expertise for *Back to the Future* run at a cool eighty-eight mph at all times. There's nobody I'd trust getting into a DeLorean with more. Period."

—Ben Bateman, movie critic and trivia champion

"Since they came out, *Back to the Future* movies have always been popular. Now with the publication of *Why We Love Back to the Future*, they are even more so, as author Brad Gilmore takes the reader behind the scenes to reveal many unknown facts and information. For instance, Michael J. Fox was the first choice for the character he played but was unable to do so until later... Gilmore has a fan's keen eye... *Why We Love Back to the Future* creates a new perspective to enhance viewing pleasure of all the flicks when viewed again."

—Midwest Book Review

"*Back to the Future* is one of my all-time favorite movies. Brad did a wonderful job of recreating the wonderful nostalgia the movie elicits, while also unearthing nuggets about the film that I didn't know. A great read that I'd recommend to all fans, young and old."

—Ariel Helwani, MMA journalist

"Brad Gilmore's *Why We Love Back to the Future* is a must-read for every *Back to the Future* fan. His passion for the iconic trilogy shines through as he dives deep into the world of Hill Valley, uncovering fascinating behind-the-scenes details and offering new insights into the beloved films. With a mix of enthusiasm and curiosity, Gilmore delivers a treasure trove of information that will leave even the most die-hard BTTF fans feeling like they've discovered something new."

—Sean Tajipour, mayor of Nerdtropolis

"Imagine a reality where Michael J. Fox didn't play Marty McFly (heavy!), or where we didn't get two sequels. There are so many interesting tidbits like these in *Why We Love Back to the Future*, but the most important part is Brad's love for the best film trilogy ever. Get ready to relive some great childhood memories with a read that will bring a smile to your face."

—Rodolfo Martinez, founder of Lucha Comics

"Brad Gilmore masterfully weaves nostalgia with fresh perspectives in this celebration of *Back to the Future*. His passion for the trilogy shines through every page, uncovering hidden gems and offering new insights that even the most devoted fans will appreciate. A must-read for anyone who has ever dreamed of hopping into a DeLorean and traveling through time."

—Claudio Mendrano, Emmy-nominated director at CW39 Houston

"The passion that Brad has for the *Back to the Future* films is so palpable through his writing that you'll want to drop everything and rewatch the trilogy again and again. Through his research and genuine fandom, he's able to shed new light on this timeless film franchise, things I had never known. A must-read for all *Back to the Future* fans, from one of the biggest fans/experts out there!"

—Michael Carrell, host of *Comicast*

"Buckle up and join Brad for a thrilling ride at eighty-eight miles per hour in this captivating exploration of the beloved *Back to the Future* trilogy. As the host of *Back to the Future: The Podcast*, Gilmore unleashes his passion and insider trivia, uncovering what makes these films modern classics. Dive into character timelines, wild fan theories, and even how the movie's predictions compare to today. This book is a must-have for any fan wanting to geek out and discover new insights about the *Back to the Future* universe!"

—Fred of Derf Designs

"Brad's love for pop culture is lifelong and his appreciation of cinema, through the lens of his own fandom, is palpable. His writing has a way of reigniting the excitement and wonder of seeing *Back to the Future* for the very first time."

—Avery Davis, award-winning musician

"It's rare a movie comes along and captivates audiences the way *Back to the Future* did. Through Brad's words, you're whisked through time as you're reminded of the deep impact the film had on your childhood and how it still resonates with new generations after all these years."

—Chalice Williams, entertainment journalist

WHY WE LOVE BACK TO THE FUTURE

WHY WE LOVE BACK TO THE FUTURE

40 Years of Fandom, Flux Capacitors, and Timeless Adventures

BRAD GILMORE

Miami

Published by Mango Publishing, a division of Mango Publishing Group, Inc.

Cover Design: Jermaine Lau & Elina Diaz
Layout & Design: Jermaine Lau & Elina Diaz
Interior Photos: Jeremy Kendrick Photo, design by Bryan Ward

For permission requests, please contact the publisher at:
Mango Publishing Group
5966 South Dixie Highway, Suite 300
Miami, FL 33143
info@mango.bz

For special orders, quantity sales, course adoptions and corporate sales, please email the publisher at sales@mango.bz. For trade and wholesale sales, please contact Ingram Publisher Services at customer.service@ingramcontent.com or +1.800.509.4887.

Why We Love Back to the Future: 40 Years of Fandom, Flux Capacitors, and Timeless Adventures

Library of Congress Cataloging-in-Publication number: 2024951664
ISBN: (print) 978-1-68481-787-0, (ebook) 978-1-68481-788-7
BISAC category code SOC022000 SOCIAL SCIENCE / Popular Culture

To my family, friends, and loved ones from
the past, present, and future—

I thank you all for your belief in me.
My love for you will last for all time.

"Take me away to where I had a kid's innocence,
'cause in a sense, that's what I've been missing ever since."

—Twenty Eleven

TABLE OF CONTENTS

FOREWORD

BY MIKEY DAY

If you're looking for a proper celebration of all things *Back to the Future*, you've come to the right book. Its author is among the truest of fans. Just how true a fan is Mr. Gilmore? The man asked me to write this foreword in a rain-damaged, old letter delivered inside a weathered Western Union portfolio. Like Brad, and most likely you, I am a full dork for the *Back to the Future* franchise. Upon arriving home after seeing *Part I* in the theater, I made a crude flux capacitor out of a shoebox and duct-taped it to my Big Wheel. And for those six seconds before the shoebox fell off and I ran over it, I *was* Marty McFly.

That was the beginning of a beautiful fan-ship. I still vividly recall going on the ride for the first time at Universal Studios. My mom later told me I had a look on my face like I was "staring into the face of God."

In my junior year of high school, a fellow fanboy and I joined the Homecoming committee solely to ensure the dance's theme would be "Enchantment Under the Sea." (We succeeded.)

On one of the first dates I went on with my now-wife, she out of nowhere quoted Lorraine's line: "Over there, on my hope chest." I believe I might've fallen in love with her that very moment. When we showed our son *Part I* for the first time, I was so happy to be sharing the experience with him that when the DeLorean backed out of Doc's truck, I fully started crying. And yes, my son thought it was kind of weird I was crying during that moment of the movie. The story, the characters, the car, the music, everything is simply perfect. I will forever be grateful to Robert Zemeckis and Bob Gale for giving us these films. And even more grateful that they have a legal contract in place preventing these films from being remade.

I'm sure that, like me, you cannot consume enough information about *Back to the Future*. So, enjoy Brad's love letter to a franchise that continues to captivate us. And when you're finished with the book, keep it somewhere special. Like your hope chest.

Happy reading, bojos.

INTRODUCTION
BY HARRY WATERS, JR.

THANK YOU FOR THE INVITATION

In January 1985, I was invited to the Enchantment Under the Sea dance. I was encouraged to play the guitar, as well as lead a band of musicians called The Starlighters. There was magic in the air, vibrating all around me, the stage, and the dance floor. A storyline was about to reach its conclusion here, enacted by a simple kiss, or the time continuum would be unwound.

Yes, Marvin Berry was offered a great opportunity to be included in the iconic and still engaging *Back to the Future*. Over the decades, this story of time travel, friendship, and fun has connected the globe in unexpected ways.

The dance, where the song "Earth Angel" brought together George McFly and Lorraine Baines, will forever be remembered. It not only united those characters but also brought together legions of fans of all ages. Rarely has a movie spoken across so many divisions and generations as this one.

During the past fifteen years, we have discovered that there are devoted fans in almost every corner of the planet—some who even learned to speak English by watching the movie over and over. *Great Scott!*

As an actor who was invited by Bob Zemeckis to portray Marvin Berry, I didn't ever see the entire script. Our twenty-minute conversation about theater gave him enough to decide I was the right fit for the role.

In the mid-1980s, the country was dealing with health crises, ongoing conflicts around the world, and cultural reimaginings. Into the midst of it all, the two Bobs—Gale and Zemeckis—crafted an imagined history of "What if?"

Like many teenagers, we often don't fully understand our parents or guardians when they were younger—except for the stories they choose to share. This script gave everyone a chance to experience a "pseudo-phenomenon" up close. It was a truly inspired embodiment through the skills of Michael J. Fox. His Marty McFly—with the puffy jacket and suspenders—will forever remind us to hold close the ones we love. In this case, Jennifer Parker is portrayed by the ineffable Claudia Wells in *Part I*. There's also the encouragement that Marty offers to the worker in the diner, Goldie Wilson, to reach for his dreams. As the song in the musical says, "You gotta start somewhere!" Donald Fullilove has shone brightly in his portrayal of Mayor Goldie Wilson, becoming a beloved character for fans across the universe.

I mention these two actors because, together, we are the supporting glue that allows us to be part of this cinematic history—a history we were invited to join, especially as we approach the fortieth anniversary in 2025.

As Shakespeare would say, "We are such stuff as dreams are made on." As Marvin Berry, I am deeply appreciative of the never-ending love for this movie and all it offers. This has been a dream we never knew could be.

Some may question the purpose of this introduction. It's simply a reminder that we are all invited to this dance. Thank you for your time and your love of time travel, and remember—you are all Earth Angels.

PART I

TIME CIRCUITS ON

PROLOGUE

GREAT SCOTT

It was the beginning of the summer of 2024. I walked out the front door of my house, ready to have a memorable experience—one I never thought would truly happen. The Houston summer was in full effect, and the humidity was inescapable. My mirrored Wayfarer glasses immediately fogged up as I put my backpack in the back of my truck and got into the front seat. I backed out of my driveway and began the thirty-five-minute commute to the George R. Brown Convention Center in Houston, Texas. I was driving to meet two icons, not only of the silver screen but also personal heroes of mine—Marty McFly and Doc Brown!

I was heading to an event called Comicpalooza, where the headlining act this year was Michael J. Fox and Christopher Lloyd. I was giddy with excitement. Although I had spoken to Christopher Lloyd on my podcast on two occasions, being able to see the man in the flesh was something I could not pass up. Having had no interactions with Michael J. Fox, I knew this moment would be heavy for a lot of reasons.

I pulled into the back of the convention center and looked into my rearview mirror, checking my appearance. It was almost as if I had the same butterflies I did the night of the Lamar High School senior prom or the ones that Marty McFly and his father shared the evening of the Enchantment Under the Sea dance, although their respective nerves couldn't have been more different. I got out of my truck and walked onto the convention center floor, astounded by the number of cosplaying Doc Browns and Marty McFlys running all around. Having not been to many comic-cons, I was overwhelmed by everything I saw—posters, props, and more.

I looked for signage to indicate where to go and checked my watch. I had about twenty minutes until the moment. As I found my location, someone asked me if I was there to meet Michael and Christopher Lloyd, and I gave a resounding yes with a big smile across my face.

I stood in line, and the line began to move, not at eighty-eight mph, but I felt as though my heart rate had already exceeded eighty-eight bpm. As I inched my way closer and closer, I turned the corner around the curtain and saw them sitting there. I don't want to say that there was something in the space-time continuum or some sort of destiny that brought us together, but it did feel like déjà vu. It felt as though I had known these people my entire life. I had spent thousands of hours discussing them, writing about them, and watching them for all thirty-one years of my life.

I looked over at the two who were posing for photographs, and Christopher Lloyd and I locked eyes for a moment. It could have been a second of recognition from our previous encounters, or he might have been thinking, "Why is this gentleman dressed in a full suit? Who is he cosplaying as?" Or maybe he thought I was going to ask him to become a subscriber of the *Saturday Evening Post.* One could not be too certain. But that single second of recognition felt as though it lasted much longer.

By the time I had gotten over the racing thoughts in my head about what I would say, what I would tell these two individuals—how much they meant to me, how much they continue to mean to me, and how much they mean to people around the world—I heard the photographer go, "Okay, ready, one, two, three...all right, thank you, next." Before I could even get a word out, the photo had been taken, and I was being ushered out of line. But I don't regret a single second of it. Now, that photo is proudly fixed to the front of my refrigerator and posted on all my social media channels as a photo I never thought would exist.

As I am writing this today, we are approaching several anniversaries related to *Back to the Future*, both publicly known and some special to me. In November 2024, we will be celebrating thirty-five years of *Back to the Future Part II*. Then in May, it will be thirty-five years of *Back to the Future Part III*, followed by a July anniversary celebrating forty years since audiences first saw "Steven Spielberg presents a Robert Zemeckis film: *Back to the Future*," the number one movie of 1985, by the way.

But there is another anniversary related to *Back to the Future* coming up. On April 14, 2025, it will be the fifth anniversary of the first edition of this very book, *Why We Love Back to the Future!* It's hard to believe that this project, which started in 2019 and was published in 2020, has already made it to its fifth birthday and is ready to enroll in kindergarten. In truth, I'm thankful for having written the original version of this book because it opened so many different doors for me personally, professionally, and *Back to the Future*-ly.

When the book was first released, several things happened. One, I reread it and realized I had made some mistakes, but that's what happens when you research, proofread, and edit a book on your own. I also realized there were several elements of the franchise that I began to know better after I published the book. So many people reached out from all over the country and even internationally with more details about these movies, with ideas that could be implemented into the book, and with minor corrections of things that I got wrong. I was so thankful that they reached out!

Throughout this book, I will reference numerous interviews I've conducted with key personalities from *Back to the Future*—whether through my radio show, TV work, or *Back to the Future: The Podcast*. For the record, none of these interviews were done specifically for this book, but their insights and stories have enriched my understanding of the franchise, and I'm excited to share them with you here. You will also read several letters in this book from my fellow friends in time. Each of these letters are from people who have been involved in the Futureverse or have been impacted by it, and I believe you will enjoy hearing from them as well.

These last five years, I've grown as an individual, a writer, an author, and a storyteller. I became less and less eager to show off my literary work. So, as we approach the five-year anniversary of the book and all these important *Back to the Future* anniversaries, I reached out to the good folks at Mango Publishing and said, "Can I do a part two? Can we retake this?" I wanted another go at it because I wanted to make the quintessential *Back to the Future* book from the fan's perspective. I wanted to truly live up to the subtitle of a celebration of the greatest time-travel story ever told. There were parts that I thought I could dive deeper into, and there were new things that came out about *Back to the Future* after the publishing of the book that I thought I could discuss; most of the book has been completely rewritten or just expanded on. I look at the original version as a great first draft; however, it provided the bones I needed to make the one you are about to read. I had interactions with so many people from the *Back to the Future* universe since the initial publishing of the book that I felt I needed to do a true second edition, an edition of this book that would make every fan and friend of the *Back to the Future* trilogy smile, raise their hand in the air, and point to the sky while simultaneously yelling, "Great Scott!"

And although the first edition of the book might not have ever been in time for school, it might not have ever been in time for dinner; this time it will be so heavy due to the overload of information that is about to occur.

So, whether you are reading this in bed, listening to this during your workout, or adjusting the brightness on your e-reader while taking a cross-continental flight, I hope you enjoy this ride through time and explore *Why We Love Back to the Future*!

HOW THE PAST BROUGHT ON THE FUTURE

June 9, 2019

Great Scott, I can't believe I am writing a book. A *book*? What in the name of Sir Isaac H. Newton is happening here!? Somebody must have been sitting too close to the Hill Valley clock tower when lightning struck and made a grave mistake. Never mind that—it's happening whether the space-time continuum wants it to or not. I am writing a book about *Back to the Future*. And it's not just any film franchise to me—it's *the* franchise.

As I write this today, June 9, the same day as Michael J. Fox's birthday, I'm thinking about how this journey began for me. How did it come to be that I would have the honor of doing a deep dive into a series that's loved worldwide? Allow me to provide some background on how this book came to be. I was hanging a clock in my bathroom in 1999 when I slipped and fell. When I came to, I had a vision...a vision of this...

Actually, I could only wish that's what happened. Here's the real story: In 1999, I was seven years old and had just gotten home to start my after-school tradition. That tradition was simple: change out of my school uniform, take my shoes off, pay no attention to any homework I had, play with my next-door neighbor, Emerson, and then go to my room. My room, for some reason, had bunk beds even though I had no siblings close to my age, and there's no way my brother (who was twenty-three years older than me) would have wanted the top bunk. But once I arrived in my little fortress of solitude, I'd find the remote and turn on the Disney Channel.

Disney Channel was awesome when I was a kid. You had *Boy Meets World*, *Lizzie McGuire*, *Even Stevens*, and other shows that I'm sure I'm forgetting. Anyhow, Disney Channel would always show a movie at seven o'clock central, but something odd happened with the schedule one fateful evening. Instead of a Disney Channel Original Movie playing, there was a marathon planned for that evening: three time-travel films I had never heard of before.

Now, let's pause there for a second. I mean, we have all the time in the world, right? Many *Back to the Future* fans will know the famous story that Bob Gale and Robert Zemeckis (the co-writers of the film) tell about pitching their idea for a time-travel story. The concept was about a boy who goes back in time and accidentally interrupts his parents' first meeting, causing his mother to fall in love with him, jeopardizing his existence in the future.

As the story goes, every studio they met with said they were looking for a raunchier 1980s comedy, and this film seemed to have too much of a soft side. The heads of all the major studios told Bob and Bob the same thing: "You know what? You should pitch this to Disney! They would love it!" So, Bob and Bob took this advice and went to Disney, who told them they were out of their minds if they thought the "House of Mouse" would ever produce a film with an incestuous relationship between a mother and her son.

And honestly, I don't blame Disney for turning them down. The plot, out of context, could sound worrisome if you didn't see the charming adventure it would eventually become. Ironically, I experienced the greatest cinematic adventure in movie history for the first time on none other than the Disney Channel.

I will never forget it. There I was, sitting on the lower bunk, when the title card flashed across the screen: "Up next, *Back to the Future.*" From the moment I heard the title, I knew I was locked in. The idea of time travel fascinated me. Then, when I saw the DeLorean time machine, Doc Brown, the iconic music, and Marty's life preserver, I entered a world where I felt at home. That night, one film led into the next, and I stayed up past my bedtime to watch the entire marathon that Bob Gale and Robert Zemeckis had dreamed up.

The next morning, thankfully a Saturday, I ran downstairs as my parents were making a sweet Southern breakfast of scrambled eggs, pigs-in-a-blanket, and grits. I excitedly told them about the phenomenal story I had seen the night before on the Disney Channel. I begged and pleaded for them to take me to the local Blockbuster so I could rent the trilogy and dive back into the world of *Back to the Future.* My mother, always supportive when she could tell I truly wanted something, obliged. We drove down to Blockbuster that very moment—or well, not exactly *that* moment. I couldn't leave those eggs just sitting there, could I?

After finishing breakfast, I entered the blue-and-yellow-clad Blockbuster, went straight to the science fiction section, and found the trilogy. Sadly, *Back to the Future Part III* had already been rented out, so I could only get parts one and two. As soon as we returned home, I grabbed a large, pink, hand-woven blanket of my grandmother's from the linen closet (which I pretended had been made in 1955) and gathered my art supplies. I went into the room with the largest television set, spread the blanket on the floor, and dumped out my bucket of colored pencils, ink pens, and crayons. I started drawing blue sparks and red lightning on sheets of white printer paper to imitate the flux capacitor at full flux.

Once I believed my calculations were correct and my version of the time machine was ready for temporal displacement, I "went eighty-eight mph" straight back to what should be the United States' capital: Hill Valley, California. And from that day on, I was obsessed.

Like many kids, when something catches your attention, you latch onto it and dive in head-first. Just as I had become obsessed with the WWF in 1998, *Back to the Future* claimed a large part of my brain's real estate. I couldn't wait to return to Edgar Allen Poe Elementary on Monday morning to tell my friends about the incredible new movies I had discovered. To my surprise, not one of them had watched the Disney Channel marathon over the weekend. Even worse, no one in Mrs. Gray's first-grade class had even *heard* of *Back to the Future.*

But before we move on, I should mention that I did my due diligence back then. I found it odd that my teacher shared her surname with a famous book of sports statistics, and I felt compelled to investigate. One day before lunch, I approached Mrs. Gray and asked if she had, in fact, written *Grays Sports Almanac.* I figured that with the year 2000 quickly approaching, it was plausible she might have penned the book that had caused Marty, Doc, and company so much trouble. Mrs. Gray, however, quickly denied any involvement. All these years later, I'm still not so sure I can take her word for it, but I've moved on.

Back to the Future became my life. Just a couple of years later, I became even more connected to the series in a way I never thought I would. Most kids, if they're lucky, have both a mom and dad in their lives, but those who have relationships with their grandparents are especially fortunate. I was one of those lucky kids. I saw my grandparents every day after school. They were more than just my mother's parents—they were like a second set of parents and two of my closest friends. That's what made my grandmother's diagnosis of Parkinson's Disease so tough.

I was only nine years old when we learned of her condition. I didn't fully understand the severity of it, but I knew what Parkinson's was because my cinematic idol, Michael J. Fox, had the same diagnosis. Over the next several years, I watched the disease take a toll on my grandmother's body. She eventually succumbed to it in 2016 after over a decade of fighting it. I share this because her diagnosis brought me even closer to these films, and Michael J. Fox became a symbol of hope for me, my family, and others affected by Parkinson's. Fox's efforts to raise awareness and funds through the Michael J. Fox Foundation for Parkinson's Research have made a tremendous impact. I support his foundation daily by wearing my "Team Fox" bracelet, which just so happens to match the colors of the *Back to the Future* logo. I will forever admire Michael J. Fox, not just for these films but for everything he does to find a cure for this terrible disease. He truly embodies his character's belief that "if you put your mind to it, you can accomplish anything."

I continued to immerse myself in the world of *Back to the Future.* With each anniversary edition release, I eagerly spent my money to get my hands on new special features and learn more about my favorite trilogy. In the months leading up to 2015—the actual year that Doc, Marty, Jennifer, and Einstein traveled to in *Back to the Future Part II*—I searched for ways to celebrate. Podcasts were booming around this time, and you could find a show covering almost anything.

There was *The Steve Austin Show* hosted by Stone Cold Steve Austin, *Seincast,* which covered all 180 episodes of *Seinfeld,* and countless other shows. But surprisingly, there was no podcast dedicated solely to *Back to the Future.* As I was already hosting my radio show in Houston and co-hosting a sports show with two-time WWE Hall of Famer Booker T, I decided that instead of waiting for someone else to create the podcast, I would take matters into my own hands. I saw an opportunity to share my love for the movies with fans all over the world. And so, *Back to the Future: The Podcast* was born.

On April 24, 2015, I launched the podcast and soon after started speaking with several people involved with the films. In the first five episodes alone, I had the incredible privilege of interviewing Claudia Wells, who portrayed Jennifer Parker in the first film, and Kevin Pike, the special effects supervisor responsible for overseeing the film's practical effects, including the iconic DeLorean time machine and various other sequences. Jeffrey Weissman, who took over the role of George McFly in *Back to the Future Part II* and *Part III* after Crispin Glover's departure, also joined me for a conversation. I couldn't believe it—I was talking to the people who had brought this trilogy to life.

The podcast began to take on a life of its own. As the episodes piled up, the special guests kept coming. I had the opportunity to speak with Stephen Wynne, owner of the DeLorean Motor Company, which led to a personal tour of the DeLorean headquarters. Harry Waters Jr., who portrayed Marvin Berry, and Stephen Clark, the executive director of BackToTheFuture.com, both graced the podcast with their stories and insights. Beyond the podcast, I've had the incredible honor of interviewing cast members and creators for my radio and TV work, including Bob Gale, Christopher Lloyd, Lea Thompson, Crispin Glover, Don Fullilove, and James Tolkan, just to name a few.

It's been amazing to connect with so many people who were a part of making these movies, but the best part has been the interaction with fans. Thousands of people from all over the world discover the podcast each year, and I'm continually blown away by the number of emails, messages, and tweets I receive from "pinheads" (as I affectionately call *Back to the Future* superfans). It's their passion and enthusiasm that have motivated me to keep pushing forward and led me to take the next step in expressing my love for the franchise: writing this book.

In this book, we will explore the full spectrum of *Back to the Future*—from how the germ of an idea transformed into a cultural phenomenon, to what happened in 2015 and how it compared to the film's version of the future. We'll debate who the best characters are, explore fan theories that have never been discussed in any book before, and dig into why these films remain so damn rewatchable. Now that all three movies—movies with "future" in their titles—are ironically set in the past, we'll break down why they still feel as relevant today as they did when they were first released. Why are they so generationally loved? Why are they so timeless?

And now, four decades after Doc Brown and Marty McFly first took us on this wild ride, I think it's finally safe to say that we're officially Back...Back from the Future.

CHAPTER 1

THE HISTORY OF HILL VALLEY

Back to the Future is, without a doubt in my mind, the greatest trilogy in the history of cinema. No other standalone series of three films has rivaled its blockbuster success, cultural impact, or enduring appeal. Some may be quick to mention *Star Wars* in response to that claim, but let's not forget there are now nine films in the Skywalker saga, which disqualifies it from being a true trilogy. *Indiana Jones* had a good shot at competing with the time-travel epic, but a fourth film was released in 2008, and a fifth installment with Harrison Ford reprising his role as the beloved archaeologist was released in 2023. Meanwhile, the Marvel Cinematic Universe (MCU) has dozens of interconnected films, and the *James Bond* franchise spans more than sixty years with twenty-five movies (and counting)—so neither of them can be considered trilogies.

That leaves *Back to the Future* with only one real competitor in the realm of true trilogies: *The Godfather* series by Francis Ford Coppola. While *The Godfather* certainly has its place in cinematic history, I still give the edge to *Back to the Future* for two key reasons. First, let's be honest—*Back to the Future Part III* is vastly superior to *The Godfather Part III*. And second, well, I am writing a book about *Back to the Future*, so I admit to a bias.

Biases aside, *Back to the Future* captured the imagination of people all over the world when it was released in July 1985. It quickly became a cultural phenomenon and ended up as the highest-grossing film of the year, surpassing major hits like *Rambo: First Blood Part II*, *Rocky IV*, *A View to a Kill*, and even another cult classic starring Christopher Lloyd, *Clue*. But how did a simple idea from writer Bob Gale, born out of a chance encounter with his father's high school yearbook, evolve into one of the most beloved and successful film franchises of all time? Well, the story of *Back to the Future*'s creation mirrors the journey of Marty McFly—starting with two friends who embark on an incredible, fantastical adventure.

Robert Zemeckis and Bob Gale first crossed paths as students in the film program at the University of Southern California (USC). Zemeckis, born on May 14, 1952, in Chicago, Illinois, had been fascinated with film and television from an early age. He often used his parents' eight-millimeter camera to film family events, birthdays, and other home movies. While watching *The Tonight Show with Johnny Carson*, Zemeckis learned about the possibility of attending film school. Inspired, he decided to chase his dream of becoming a Hollywood filmmaker and enrolled in USC's prestigious film program.

Gale, born on May 25,1951 in University City, Missouri, had an equally strong passion for storytelling, though his early love was for comic books. As a teenager, he created a comic series called *The Green Vomit* and founded a comic book club in his hometown of St. Louis. Gale's love for movies grew alongside his passion for comics, and he eventually set his sights on becoming a writer. His path led him to USC, where he would meet his future creative partner, Zemeckis. The two quickly bonded over their shared enthusiasm for big, mainstream Hollywood movies.

Not long after they became friends, Zemeckis and Gale started collaborating on various projects. One of their first joint efforts was a script titled *Bordello of Blood*, a film about vampire prostitutes that they hoped would be their first produced project. Although the film didn't get made at the time (it was later turned into a TV movie for *Tales from the Crypt*), the duo realized how much they enjoyed working together and decided to continue writing as a team.

Their next step was television. They landed an opportunity to write for a short-lived horror series called *Kolchak: The Night Stalker*, which starred Darren McGavin as a newspaper reporter investigating mysterious crimes. Despite lasting only one season, *Kolchak* left its mark on genre TV, and the episode that Zemeckis and Gale wrote, titled "Chopper," remains a fun watch for fans of horror and sci-fi. While *Kolchak* didn't give the duo their big break, it was a valuable experience that taught them the ins and outs of writing for television—and set the stage for the bigger projects to come.

With an official writing credit to their names, Bob Gale and Robert Zemeckis gained momentum in the entertainment industry. Their collaboration continued with writing for television, contributing scripts to shows like *McCloud* and *Get Christie Love!*—a popular detective series featuring one of the first African American female leads on television. Their chemistry as a writing duo was undeniable, and their collective talents soon caught the attention of NBC executives. The network offered each of them a lucrative seven-year contract worth $50,000 annually to write television shows. For two up-and-coming screenwriters, this was a golden opportunity. However, Gale and Zemeckis had bigger dreams than television. They wanted to break into the world of feature films, so they took the offer to their new entertainment lawyers, who, surprisingly, advised them to turn it down.

The Bobs followed their instincts. They knew their hearts were in movies, not TV, so they set their sights on Hollywood. One key figure in this journey was a young director Zemeckis had met during a visit to USC—none other than Steven Spielberg. At that time, Spielberg wasn't yet the Hollywood titan he would soon become, but he was already well on his way to stardom.

Spielberg visited the USC campus to screen his film *The Sugarland Express*, a crime drama that had garnered critical praise. After the screening, Zemeckis, impressed by Spielberg's work, boldly approached him and asked if he would be willing to watch his short film, *A Field of Honor*, which had won a Student Academy Award. Spielberg agreed, and the two watched the film together in Spielberg's office. That meeting marked the beginning of a long-standing professional relationship and friendship between Zemeckis, Gale, and Spielberg.

It wasn't long before Spielberg would direct a script written by the Bobs: *1941*, a World War II comedy. As Spielberg's follow-up to *Jaws* and *Close Encounters of the Third Kind*, expectations for *1941* were high, but the film ultimately underperformed at the box office. The ambitious comedy didn't resonate with audiences, and Spielberg considered it a misstep. However, Spielberg's faith in Zemeckis and Gale didn't waver. He recognized their talent and continued to champion their work, becoming executive producer on two of Zemeckis's early directorial efforts: *I Wanna Hold Your Hand* (1978) and *Used Cars* (1980), both written by Gale and Zemeckis.

I Wanna Hold Your Hand was a lighthearted comedy about the excitement surrounding The Beatles' first visit to the United States, while *Used Cars* was a raucous satire about a scheming car salesman, starring Kurt Russell. Neither film was a huge box office success, but they both demonstrated the Bobs' knack for crafting engaging and original stories. *Used Cars* earned the attention of Frank Price.

Used Cars received the highest score in a test screening that Frank Price, the film executive at Columbia Pictures, had ever seen during his tenure. Price, like both Bob Gale and Robert Zemeckis, was a Midwesterner, but by the time he was running Columbia, he was more than just another studio executive in a suit. His career began in 1951 as a story editor and writer for several television shows under the CBS banner. For nearly a decade,.he worked on various TV projects until he met Sid Sheinberg (who, coincidentally, would later have a significant influence on *Back to the Future*) and made the transition into becoming a studio executive. Price then worked for Universal TV as senior vice president until 1978, when he was hired to become the president of Columbia Pictures.

During his leadership at Columbia, Price oversaw a slate of critically and commercially successful films. These included *Kramer vs. Kramer, The Karate Kid,* and *Ghostbusters.* If not for Frank Price, *Ghostbusters* might have been called *Ghostbreakers.* The title "*Ghostbusters*" was legally restricted by the 1970s children's show *The Ghost Busters,* but Price helped the film studio secure the rights to the name. Price had a reputation for recognizing potential, and when he saw the test screening results for *Used Cars,* he knew Gale and Zemeckis were talents worth backing. Price knew there was more to come from the Bobs.

Meanwhile, Gale and Zemeckis were determined to come up with a compelling time-travel story, but they struggled to find the right hook. According to Gale, as shared in the *Tales from the Future: In the Beginning* featurette on the *Back to the Future 30th Anniversary Edition* DVD set, inspiration struck during a visit to his parents in Missouri. At the time, Gale was on a press tour for *Used Cars*. During his visit, he discovered his father's high school yearbook in the basement. While thumbing through its decades-old pages, he learned something surprising: his father had been the president of his graduating class.

This revelation made Gale reflect on the differences between himself and his father. Gale had never been interested in high school leadership, and he imagined that if he and his father had been in school at the same time, they might not have been friends. This thought stuck with him. When Gale returned to California, he shared the story with Zemeckis. Together, they realized they had found the hook they'd been searching for: a story about a boy who travels back in time and meets his parents in high school.

Frank Price had told the Bobs to pitch their film ideas to him first. With that encouragement, Gale and Zemeckis set up a meeting and pitched the concept of a boy who goes back in time, attends high school with his parents, and accidentally makes his mother fall in love with him instead of his father. Price loved the idea and quickly inked a deal for two drafts of what would become *Back to the Future*.

Gale and Zemeckis worked quickly on their new concept and came up with a draft to pitch to Price. While the basic structure was familiar, the details were quite different from the *Back to the Future* we know today. In this draft, Marty McFly, a video pirate running a black-market operation, travels back to 1952 with Professor Brown (and his chimpanzee, Shemp), where Marty's mother, Eileen, falls for him—and Marty's challenge was to get his parents to fall in love at the "Springtime in Paris" dance.

While Price still loved the concept, he felt it needed more work. Undeterred, Gale and Zemeckis returned to their office and began rewriting the script. They employed what Gale called the "index card method" of plotting, a technique in which they would write major story points on index cards and arrange them on a bulletin board. For instance, they had the idea that Marty would "invent" rock 'n' roll in the past, so they placed one card reading "Marty plays rock 'n' roll" before the card that read "Marty invents rock 'n' roll." This method helped them organize the plot and ensure that the story flowed logically.

In the spring of 1981, Bob Gale and Robert Zemeckis completed their second draft of *Back to the Future* and eagerly presented it to Frank Price, the president of Columbia Pictures. Price, who had supported the project from the beginning, liked this version much more than the first. However, he still had reservations. At the time, teen comedies that pushed boundaries—raunchier, edgier films like *Porky's* and *Animal House*—were drawing big crowds. By comparison, *Back to the Future* was seen as a sweet, nostalgic love story wrapped in a sci-fi adventure, and Price wasn't sure if it would appeal to the same demographic. Reluctantly, Columbia passed on the project.

Despite the setback, the Bobs weren't ready to give up. They knew they had something special, and they were determined to find a studio that would take a chance on their time-traveling adventure. They began pitching *Back to the Future* to several major studios, hoping to spark interest. But they were met with a recurring question: "Is Spielberg involved?" By this time, Spielberg was Hollywood's golden boy, thanks to his massive successes with *Jaws, Close Encounters of the Third Kind,* and *Raiders of the Lost Ark*. His name carried significant weight in the industry, and many studios were hesitant to commit to the project without his involvement.

At this point, Spielberg had read the script and expressed interest in coming on board as a producer. He loved the story, calling it a fun, unique take on familiar themes like family, growing up, and finding your place in the world. Spielberg's instincts told him that the project had real potential. However, Zemeckis and Gale were conflicted. They deeply respected Spielberg and appreciated his support, but they were determined to prove themselves without relying on his influence. The Bobs were conscious of the fact that, up until then, they had been closely associated with Spielberg's projects, and they worried that if *Back to the Future* failed with Spielberg's name attached, they would be written off as merely his protégés.

Understanding their desire to stand on their own, Spielberg graciously stepped back, allowing the Bobs to continue their search for a studio. As the rejections piled up, Zemeckis realized he needed to prove his worth as a director if they were ever going to get *Back to the Future* off the ground. His chance came when he was offered the opportunity to direct *Romancing the Stone* (1984), a romantic adventure comedy starring Michael Douglas, Kathleen Turner, and Danny DeVito.

Zemeckis poured everything he had into *Romancing the Stone*, fully aware that the film's success or failure would determine the future of his career. If the film flopped, *Back to the Future* would never get made. But if it succeeded, Hollywood would have no choice but to take him seriously as a director.

Romancing the Stone turned out to be a massive hit, both critically and financially, earning over $75 million at the domestic box office and solidifying Zemeckis as a bankable filmmaker. Gene Siskel, one-half of the legendary film critic duo Siskel & Ebert, spoke highly of *Romancing the Stone*, even though he wasn't a fan of its title:

> So many of its elements are so fresh and funny. And the relationship between Kathleen Turner and Michael Douglas is so genuine and unpredictable. *Romancing the Stone*, despite its dumb title, gets a thumbs up from me. I appreciated everything that was fresh in this film while watching it. I knew that someone was trying to entertain me, and that's very important.

One of the stars of *Romancing the Stone*, Michael Douglas, recalled observing Zemeckis's work on set and his unique directing style. In an interview for *Rekindling the Romance*, a retrospective on the film, Douglas said:

> A great vision by Bob Zemeckis. You could now see the talent that this guy had and what he was going to do.

Kathleen Turner, the other star of the film, also praised Zemeckis's vision, stating:

> He sees things wonderfully, and I think he has a tremendous sense of the build of the film.

Zemeckis's sense of visuals and storytelling later influenced one of his future *Back to the Future* cast members, Lea Thompson. When I spoke to Lea in 2020, while she was promoting an episode of *The Goldbergs* she directed, she mentioned how she often incorporates Robert Zemeckis's directing style into her own work:

> A lot of times I really do reference Bob Zemeckis, who directed me in *Back to the Future* Parts I, II, and III. He had a really great eye for filling up the frame with content. You can watch *Back to the Future* a bunch of times and see a bunch of different things.

> I try to do that—I try to put as much story as I can in every shot, and so I kind of use his template.

Bob Z's reputation skyrocketed almost overnight, and the doors of Hollywood began to swing open. Suddenly, the same studios that had passed on *Back to the Future* were eager to get a piece of the action. Offers came pouring in, but the Bobs knew exactly who they wanted to partner with. They returned to the one person who had believed in the project from the beginning: Steven Spielberg. Spielberg, now fully on board as an executive producer, was thrilled to help bring *Back to the Future* to life. The team that had been working together since the days of *I Wanna Hold Your Hand* and *Used Cars* was reunited, and with Zemeckis' newfound directorial clout, the film finally had the backing it needed.

The band was officially back together, and this time, the stakes were higher than ever. The Bobs knew they had something special in their time-travel story, and with Spielberg by their side, they were ready to create a film that would not only captivate audiences but stand the test of time. Little did they know, *Back to the Future* was about to become a cultural touchstone and one of the most beloved trilogies in cinema history.

What began as a simple "what if" question about a father and son going to high school together was about to evolve into the most iconic time-travel story of all time.

LETTERS FROM YOUR FRIENDS IN TIME: ROXY STRIAR

Actress

I grew up with a big brother. Anyone reading this who grew up with an older sibling knows that, as the baby, it takes *a lot to* earn cool points. My brother was into sports, so I was into sports (Jason Kidd was my favorite player because I thought his last name sounded cool). My brother loved video games, so I loved video games (though I could never figure out which button did what, and he kicked my butt every time). My brother loved wrestling, so I loved wrestling (even though I was the human guinea pig for replicating all the moves he saw).

My brother was the coolest person in the world to me. Wanna guess who was the coolest person in the world to him? Of course, it was Marty McFly. From the vest to the hoverboard, Marty had swag. My brother even dressed as Marty for Halloween. So, naturally, we had all three VHS tapes at home and would watch *Back to the Future I, II,* and *III* back-to-back-to-back. My brother once told me, "The law states that the oldest sibling always gets to choose what the kids watch," and I believed him. I wasn't about to risk going to prison at age five over controlling the VCR.

The truth was, though, I didn't want to change the channel. I had become as obsessed with *Back to the Future* as he had. He loved the sci-fi and action; I loved the romance and comedy. He loved the cool car; I loved the...cool car too. Seriously, to this day, the DeLorean is the coolest car I've ever seen, and anyone who says otherwise is a liar. The *Fast and the Furious* movies wish their cars were that cool.

The best part about the franchise, though, is that it's truly for everyone. Every friend we had over wanted to watch *Back to the Future*. If my parents walked into the room while it was on, they would stay until the end. And now that my brother has a baby on the way, *Back to the Future* is one of the movies he can't wait to introduce to his soon-to-be daughter. Maybe one day, she'll love the movies so much that she'll convince her baby sibling they need to watch them on repeat—by law.

It's time for me to make like a tree and get out of here, but I'll leave you with this: the *Back to the Future* franchise is time-traveling timelessness at its finest. The characters, the quotability, the music—simply perfect. Most importantly, though, those movies allowed me to win major cool points with my big bro, and for that, I will forever be grateful.

Your Friend in Time,
Roxy Striar

CHAPTER 2

THIS IS HEAVY

Now in production under the Universal Pictures and Amblin Entertainment umbrella, the project was officially underway. With Universal executive Sid Sheinberg overseeing the process, the *Back to the Future* team now faced the crucial task of casting the film's key roles, but Sheinberg did have a few suggestions he wanted to make. First, he didn't like the name Eileen and suggested Lorraine—the name of his wife who had worked with Steven Spielberg and the Bobs previously on *1941*. He also wanted to change Professor Brown to "Doc" Brown and to change Shemp the chimp to Einstein the dog. All were solid suggestions that the Bobs had no problem implementing. This would not be the last of Sheinberg's requests, but these were the first and foremost notes to address.

Now that casting had begun, the producers had to find the perfect actor to play the lead role of Marty McFly. The producers and casting agents conducted an exhaustive search, according to Frank Marshall, who served as an executive producer on the film alongside Spielberg and Kathleen Kennedy. Marshall said that every young actor in Hollywood wanted to play the rock-and-roll-loving teen.

At the same time the producers were searching for the perfect Marty, a Canadian-born actor named Michael J. Fox was working on a film called *Teen Wolf*. Fox was a familiar face to filmgoers, as he portrayed Alex P. Keaton in the wildly popular Gary Goldberg-created television show *Family Ties*. While filming *Teen Wolf* in Pasadena, California, Michael J. Fox had heard a location scouting crew was just down the road working on the new Spielberg-produced time-travel film. Fox recalls being covered in his wolf costume and feeling miserable. When Michael learned his friend Crispin Glover had been tapped to be in the film, he was happy for Crispin but couldn't help but want to be in the film instead of having rubber and hair glued to his face daily.

Michael J. Fox was unaware he was indeed the first choice of the filmmakers to play McFly, but they were told he could not do the film given his commitment to *Family Ties*. After begging Goldberg to allow Fox to do both the movie and the TV show, Goldberg told them there was just no way. According to Zemeckis, the filmmakers had a deadline to cast, shoot, edit, and produce the film. If they could not meet that deadline, the entire movie would be canceled. With their backs against the wall and their first choice unavailable, the producers continued their search for the perfect Marty McFly. Johnny Depp, Ben Stiller, Jon Cryer, C. Thomas Howell, and John Cusack were all considered for the role, but ultimately, actor Eric Stoltz was cast as Marty McFly. Stoltz, still young in his career, was a talented actor. Bob Z. was sure that he could make his story work with Stoltz.

One of the abovementioned actors who auditioned for the role, Jon Cryer, went on to have a great career. For today's audiences, Jon is best known as Alan on the hit series *Two and a Half Men*, which ran for twelve seasons on CBS. He also starred as Lenny Luthor, the nephew of Lex Luthor, in *Superman IV: The Quest for Peace*, and eventually portrayed Lex Luthor in the CW Arrowverse, appearing in shows like *Supergirl*, *Batwoman*, *The Flash*, *Arrow*, and *Legends of Tomorrow*.

In 2024, while Jon was promoting his new TV series *Extended Family*, I had the chance to speak with him on my radio show. I asked him what he remembered about his audition for *Back to the Future*, and he shared some fascinating insights:

> The *Back to the Future* that I read was an earlier draft of it that had a very different ending. The Time Machine was not a DeLorean; it had a secret formula, and it turns out that the secret formula was Coca-Cola. Actually, you can find a PDF of this script floating around if you do some searches. It also had a whole different final sequence where, because it needed enough power—instead of getting power from a lightning bolt—it needed power from a nuclear explosion. So, it was Marty sneaking onto a nuclear test site in 1955 and waiting for the bomb to go off. And actually, there's a whole sequence in there where he hides in a refrigerator, which Spielberg later borrowed for *Indiana Jones and the Kingdom of the Crystal Skull*. It's so interesting to read it because it's a really fun script. You can see why Spielberg wanted to do it, but you're like, "Wow, they made a bunch of changes." They really went nuts with this thing. This isn't the movie I read for.

Although the final draft doesn't include Coca-Cola and we end up seeing the rival soda brand, Pepsi, in *Back to the Future Part II*, what Jon Cryer is saying is indeed true! In the first draft of *Back to the Future*, dated February 24, 1981, there is an early scene where Marty helps the then-"Professor" Brown discover the needed fizzy fuel to make time travel possible.

In this scene, Marty enters Professor Brown's quarters, a cluttered space where the professor is sleeping on a cot. Marty grabs a Coke from the fridge and accidentally knocks an orange under the cot, where he discovers a crate marked "Extreme Danger! Radioactive Plutonium." Nervously, he moves the orange away from the crate and tosses it in the trash.

Marty then interacts with the professor's pet monkey, Shemp, before inspecting a series of old blueprints for inventions, including a Power Converter. Unable to resist, Marty pours some Coca-Cola into the Power Converter, causing it to spark, which awakens Professor Brown. Curious, the professor tests the device, and after pouring more Coke into it, the Power Converter lights up and eventually overloads, stunning the professor. Amazed by the reaction, Brown takes the Power Converter into a locked room, leaving Marty to wonder what will happen next.

Speaking of the Professor, the next task the filmmakers had was to cast the second lead role in the film—the role of the newly named "Doc" Brown. Just as with Marty, several big-name actors were considered for the role of the crackpot scientist. Among the names being tossed around to play Emmett Brown were Jeff Goldblum, Gene Hackman, John Cleese, Michael Keaton, Gene Wilder, Chevy Chase, Steve Martin, and Eddie Murphy.

A producer working on the film, Neil Canton, suggested the actor Christopher Lloyd, who many people knew from his role as Jim Ignatowski on the television series *Taxi*. Lloyd was sent the script while filming a movie in Mexico but largely disregarded it. At the time, Lloyd had feared that he made the wrong choice leaving New York for Los Angeles and was considering going back to the Big Apple to be a stage actor. Lloyd's then-wife encouraged him to read the script and to "never leave a stone unturned." After Lloyd read the script, he called his agent and told him to set up a meeting with Robert Zemeckis.

When Chris first entered the room, the *Romancing the Stone* director knew he was a perfect fit.

Marty and Doc were without a doubt the two most important roles to cast, but arguably the third most important would be the resident bully of Hill Valley, Biff Tannen. The actor who stood apart from the rest was Tom Wilson, a young comedian who had yet to be a part of a big studio movie, let alone one being produced by Spielberg. Wilson was discovered by Judy Taylor, a casting director who said that the role of Biff was the most difficult role to cast, aside from Marty McFly. She said she spotted Wilson in a room where he was waiting to audition for another project. She called Wilson's agent on the spot and after he auditioned, he was cast as Biff Tannen. Wilson was fantastic in the role, and his subsequent performances as members of the Tannen family proved his range as an actor. We will look more into the character of Biff in a later chapter, but when you watch these films again, appreciate how good Wilson truly is in all three.

Finding Lorraine McFly didn't prove to be as challenging as casting Marty or Biff. As soon as the filmmakers discovered Lea Thompson, their search for the McFly matriarch ended. Thompson had already made a name for herself in Hollywood, and at the time, she was working on a film with Eric Stoltz. Coincidentally, Stoltz being casted as Marty in the film is what Thomas believes played a part in her being called in for an audition. Everything clicked for her when she embodied Lorraine during the tryout. Thompson's performance was a perfect balance of the sweet yet disillusioned character that Lorraine was intended to be.

Lea recalls that her first scene in the film was the family dinner scene, where the McFly family is sitting down to an awkward meal. It was here that Thompson realized she had to nail both the comedic timing and the underlying sadness that the character felt about her life. Lorraine, once filled with youthful hopes and dreams, had become a disillusioned, downtrodden housewife. Thompson credits Bob Zemeckis's direction for helping her navigate the tone of the scene. Zemeckis had an incredible ability to guide his actors through the shifts between humor and depth, ensuring that the audience could laugh at Lorraine's quirks but also empathize with her struggles.

Casting George McFly, the bumbling father of Marty, was equally pivotal to the film's dynamic. Crispin Glover, a second-generation actor from California, was ultimately the perfect choice. Crispin's father, Bruce Glover, was a notable figure in Hollywood, best known for his role as the villainous Mr. Wint in the 1971 James Bond film *Diamonds Are Forever*. Crispin, like his father, had a unique screen presence. Bob Gale recalls that Glover's distinct, almost odd way of speaking and his peculiar mannerisms instantly made him stand out. Gale later reflected, "When we saw Crispin, we just knew—he *was* George McFly. There was no question." His portrayal of George as a nervous, socially awkward pushover provided the perfect counterbalance to Marty's youthful energy and Lorraine's melancholic resignation.

In 2019, I had the chance to interview Crispin for his film *Lucky Day* on my radio show. During our conversation I wanted to ask him about his portrayal of George McFly and specifically the physicality of the character whilst delivering the lines. But just as I reached the point in the interview where I was about to ask about *Back to the Future*, something strange happened: the phone call dropped. *Great Scott!* I began to panic. I thought I had lost my chance to ask Crispin Glover about one of the most iconic performances in cinematic history.

I frantically tried dialing the number back, but it went straight to voicemail. I sat for a few minutes in despair, imagining that I'd missed my opportunity. Then, my phone rang. It was Crispin Glover, back on the line. This was my chance to finally ask him about George McFly—why he approached the character the way he did—and to delve into what made his portrayal so unique. Crispin has always brought an individualistic style to his performances, and in *Back to the Future*, his physical movements were just as memorable.

Here's what Crispin shared:

> Anything that has the psychology underneath, whether a character is overcompensating for something...or what it is that the character is going through psychologically, can certainly manifest itself not just in the words you're saying, but of course in your entire body. I definitely did work on that when working on *Back to the Future*. I try to figure that out in virtually any character that I play. Some characters end up being more physically apparent than others. It just depends on what the character is, and I do remember specifically working on psychological aspects that would manifest in that character in *Back to the Future*.

Wendie Jo Sperber was cast as Linda McFly, Marty's sister. Sperber had a long-standing relationship with both Bob Gale and Bob Zemeckis, having previously worked with them on *I Wanna Hold Your Hand* and *Used Cars*. Her familiarity with the filmmakers and her natural comedic talent made her a seamless fit for the McFly family. Sperber's dynamic on-screen chemistry with Marc McClure, who played her brother, Dave McFly, further solidified the sibling relationship. McClure, who had also worked with Zemeckis and Gale on their earlier projects, was perhaps best known at the time for his role as Jimmy Olsen in the *Superman* films alongside Christopher

Reeve. He fondly recalled his instant connection with Sperber, saying that from the moment they met, they felt like real siblings. Their playful, close bond mirrored their on-screen relationship, adding an extra layer of authenticity to the McFly family dynamic.

Claudia Wells was another young actress brought into the fold, originally cast as Marty's girlfriend, Jennifer Parker. Wells had previously auditioned for several projects under the Amblin Entertainment banner. Although she didn't land roles in those films, she was thrilled when she finally secured a part in *Back to the Future.*

Claudia was one of the very first people in the Futureverse that I had the opportunity to interview for my podcast in 2015. What a lovely and warm spirit she was then and still is now. When I asked her what she remembered about landing the role as Jennifer, here's what she shared:

> Well, I had actually done about fifty different shows before that. I started in six television series, a ton of episodic shows, movies of the week, school break specials, and commercials. I came very close to getting the lead role in *Gremlins, Goonies,* and *Young Sherlock Holmes*—all Amblin productions. I literally got down to me and one or two other girls for each role. So, by the time I walked into my *Back to the Future* audition, I was standing in front of Steven Spielberg, Bob Gale, Bob Zemeckis, Neil Canton—all the big guys. I just walked in and said, "Hey, it's me again." At that point, I had no expectations about it. I just figured I'd probably almost get it—and then I got it. That's how it happened. Now, in hindsight, I *prefer* that *Back to the Future* was the role I was cast in over any of the others. It was such a beautiful experience, being part of that movie, and the worldwide love I receive from it is something truly special.

However, as fate would have it, Wells had also filmed a pilot for ABC called *Off the Rack*. When the show was unexpectedly picked up, she had to make the difficult decision to drop out of *Back to the Future*. This led to the casting of Melora Hardin as Jennifer Parker, filling the role of Marty's love interest.

James Tolkan, known for his sharp, no-nonsense demeanor, was cast as Mr. Strickland, Hill Valley High School's tough-as-nails disciplinarian. His portrayal of the slacker-hating Strickland became iconic, embodying the strict authority figure every teenager dreaded encountering.

In 2021, I had the privilege of speaking with James Tolkan for my podcast. I reached out to him through old-fashioned snail mail, writing a letter signed "your friend in time." I'll never forget the moment when, in the middle of the NBA Finals, I received a call from James! A few weeks later, he joined the podcast and shared the story of how he landed the iconic role of Mr. Strickland:

> I got a call from Robert Zemeckis when I was doing Glengarry Glen Ross, the David Mamet play on Broadway, and that was a very special experience. But I got a call from Zemeckis and he asked me to come do *Back to the Future*. I didn't know about *Back to the Future*; I didn't know who he was. And I said, I've always said, I'm never going to Hollywood until they send for me. I figured this was my chance. I found out that I was the only actor in *Back to the Future* who did not audition, which I think means he must have seen me in something and thought I was okay. So, he hired me, and I went out to do *Back to the Future*.

Another memorable performance came from Don Fullilove, who portrayed Mayor Goldie Wilson.

In 2021, I spoke to Don Fullilove on my podcast and asked him about his start in show business.

> The first thing I ever did was voice Michael Jackson on The *Jackson 5* cartoon show. From there, I went on to do a bunch of other animated series, including *Emergency +4*, which was based on the live action TV show *Emergency!* that was on at the time. I also worked on *Kid Power*, which was based on a comic strip, along with various other radio spots and projects.

When I asked Don how it felt playing Michael Jackson and being the voice of such an iconic figure, he remarked: "I was the coolest kid in the seventh grade."

Don went on to recount his first meeting with the filmmakers of *Back to the Future*:

> Well, I don't know about most of the people from the cast. I think it was quite a few of the people from the cast. There was never a script. There was only a meeting—there was no script, there were no sides. I just went in for a meeting with them, and they were asking me questions that, until I did the film, I didn't understand what they were asking me about.
>
> They asked me if I knew how to sing, obviously, because they were probably considering the role of Marvin Berry for me as well. And I guess after the meeting, they decided, *You know what? You're a better fit as Goldie Wilson.* So, I never heard from them for—I guess, I don't know—a couple of weeks. And then I got a call, and the part was offered to me.

> Back then, video games were just becoming the rage—the arcade-style video games. And I remember going into Universal Studios, and at that time—probably still now, I'm sure—Amblin Entertainment had a compound on the Universal Studios lot. So, you're on the Universal Studios lot, and then you drive up to Amblin, and it's a whole 'nother giant gate.
>
> And as the gate—the Amblin gate—opened and you begin to see the Amblin compound, you kind of get overwhelmed because you're like, *Holy cow, this is where Steven Spielberg does all his stuff?* So, I get inside, and I remember, prior to going into the office meeting with them, there was a room just full of arcade video games to play.
>
> That was young Don's first impression of his first meeting for *Back to the Future.*

Fullilove's portrayal of Wilson, Hill Valley's optimistic and charismatic mayor, left a lasting impression, with his line, "I'm gonna clean up this town!" becoming an unforgettable moment in the film. Equally iconic was his delivery of the line "Maaayorrrr!" when his character first dreams of a political future.

Rounding out the ensemble was Harry Waters Jr., who brought charisma and soul to his role as Marvin Berry, the crooning lead singer of The Starlighters. Waters' rendition of "Earth Angel" during the Enchantment Under the Sea dance became one of the film's most iconic musical moments, marking the moment when Marty's future hung in the balance.

In a 2015 podcast interview with Waters, I spoke to him about what he remembered from getting the audition to filming on the set. Below is what he shared with me:

> I got a call from the casting director to come in because they were looking for people to sing for this movie. They said it was going to be a sort of doo-wop singer.
>
> At the time I got the audition, I was performing in a musical called *The Me Nobody Knows*, which was originally done in the seventies, and they were doing a remake in L.A. I was the oldest teenager in the world, but that's okay—I could still play them. So, I took my song in, auditioned, and then went back to rehearsal.
>
> The next day, they told me they wanted to bring me back for a callback. I thought, *Oh, great!* The callback was at Steven Spielberg's Amblin Studios, which is his own studio in the middle of Universal.
>
> It's all based on *E.T.*—it's like its own little planet. So, I go back for the callback, and it's just to sit and meet Robert Zemeckis. We talked about theater, we talked about life, we talked about being in New York and moving back to L.A.—and that was it. I left thinking, *I guess that went well.*
>
> Now, at the same time, I was also up for a TV series called *He's the Mayor*, and my agent was trying to tell me that I should wait and hold out for the TV series. I told her, *Let's wait and see what happens.*
>
> Then I got the call for *Back to the Future*, and my agent still wanted me to wait for this TV series. I said, "Wait—it's a

> Spielberg movie. I don't know what it is, but I want to be in it." So, I took the movie. I didn't get the TV series, even though I was a finalist.
>
> And when we got to filming, the best part about shooting the "Enchantment Under the Sea" dance scene was that it was the first *new* thing the entire crew was shooting. You probably know that story, I would hope.

The story that Mr. Waters was referring to is one that needs to be told indeed.

Once the film was in production, Zemeckis was set to finish in time for the studio's deadline, but there was a major problem with the film. After weeks of shooting, Zemeckis showed Spielberg some of the footage he had shot. After the two men sat in Spielberg's office, Zemeckis voiced his concern that Eric Stoltz wasn't hitting the jokes the way Zemeckis expected. Bob Z. told his friend that he didn't think Stoltz had the comedic sensibilities needed for the film and was causing the picture to fall flat. Zemeckis needed Marty McFly to deliver the jokes while still having a sense of urgency and fear of his situation. Stoltz was great for the latter portion of that description but not the former. Spielberg agreed with Zemeckis, and the decision was made to stop production and replace Stoltz.

I can remember scouring the internet, reading books, and looking through magazines, trying to find some insight on how Eric Stoltz felt about being let go from his duties as Marty McFly. At this point in his career, it would have been the biggest movie he had ever been a part of, and it went on to become one of the biggest movies of all time.

I was never able to interview Eric Stoltz myself or find an interview where he spoke openly about the experience—until one day, an old clip surfaced on YouTube. It was from Later with Bob Costas, a late-night interview show, where Stoltz was being interviewed by Costas on June 16, 1993.

At the time, Stoltz was there to promote his off-Broadway play *Down the Road.* However, during their conversation, Bob Costas brought up *Back to the Future* and asked Eric about his experience being let go from the film.

Below is a transcript of their exchange:

> **BOB:** Is it true that you had the Michael J. Fox role in *Back to the Future*?
>
> **ERIC:** Yes, it is.
>
> **BOB:** What happened?
>
> **ERIC:** Well, I used to have a great answer for this—that in the sequels, they would go back in time to the point when I was in the cast, and it would all be explained. But I can no longer give that answer. What happened was the director fired me.
>
> **BOB:** Why?
>
> **ERIC:** He didn't like my work.
>
> **BOB:** So were they well into filming, or was it right at the start?

ERIC: We were pretty far into filming, yes. He was very nice about it—well, as nice as you can be when you're firing someone. But he said that I wasn't giving the performance he wanted for his film, which I can respect.

BOB: How big of a disappointment was that for you? You had to have had a pretty good sense that this was going to be a box office success.

ERIC: No, actually, I didn't. And I try not to think about how a film might perform at the box office—I think that's detrimental to performing. But it was devastating to me. I was a young actor. It was probably the worst thing that could happen to you in your career.

BOB: Do you ever get over—when I say you, I don't mean just you individually—Does any performer, you think, ever get over the fear of being rejected by a director, by a casting director, by the audience, by critics?

ERIC: Sure, I think you do. I think people do constantly, if they're at all healthy. I have, just in the sense that—once you've been fired from a huge boffo movie, what could be worse? What could happen to me in my career that would be worse than that? And somehow, I survived it. Now, I have a much better sense of myself, and I no longer have a lot of those fears that I once did.

BOB: So, probably a good thing that it happened?

ERIC: Ultimately, yes. Difficult medicine at the time.

Everyone in the film was saddened by Stoltz's departure, as many of the actors thought he was lovely and talented. Spielberg and the filmmakers went to Sheinberg and asked if he could extend their deadline and allow them to recast the main role. Sid agreed, and the *Back to the Future* crew went back to their first choice to see if they could get Michael J. Fox to join the project.

The filmmakers, determined to cast Michael J. Fox as their lead, reached out to Gary Goldberg, creator and executive producer of *Family Ties*. They needed to convince him to allow Fox to juggle his commitment to the sitcom with filming *Back to the Future*. Initially, Goldberg was hesitant, knowing how essential Fox was to *Family Ties*, but after some persistent persuasion, he agreed to give the script to Fox with one condition: if Fox liked it, he would give his blessing for him to take the role, provided *Family Ties* remained the priority.

Goldberg called Fox into his office, handing him a large manila envelope with the *Back to the Future* script sealed inside. He instructed Fox to read it and come back with his thoughts. However, Fox didn't even need to read it. Without opening the envelope, he immediately handed it back and said, "I love it. It's the best thing I've ever read." This quick decision spoke volumes about Fox's enthusiasm, and Goldberg allowed him to take the role—on the condition that *Family Ties* would always come first. With that agreement in place, Fox was free to become Marty McFly and the filmmakers were overjoyed to finally have their perfect lead.

During an appearance at Rhode Island Comic Con in 2017, Christopher Lloyd recalled his feelings when Eric Stoltz was let go by saying:

> They asked us to come back after lunch, which was around one a.m. Everyone was there—Spielberg, Bob Gale—and then they made the announcement that Eric Stoltz was being replaced by Michael J. Fox. I was like, "Oh my God." I felt like every day on set was a "maybe day" at that point. I was still trying to find my bearings with Doc Brown and was putting so much into every shot for six weeks. And now, I thought, *Oh my God, I've got to do it all over again.*

However, things worked out for Doc Brown as he continued to say, "I didn't have to redo every shot, but it became immediately apparent that the chemistry with Michael just suddenly came alive."

Meanwhile, as production geared up again after Eric Stoltz's departure, a stroke of luck came with the casting of Marty's love interest, Jennifer Parker. Claudia Wells, who had originally been cast but had to drop out due to her commitment to the ABC series *Off the Rack*, found herself with unexpected free time when the sitcom was canceled after just six episodes. This cleared the way for Wells to step back into the role of Jennifer. Melora Hardin, who had been cast after Wells' departure, was unfortunately several inches taller than Fox, which created a noticeable height discrepancy. With the cancellation of *Off the Rack*, Wells reclaimed the role, and the production team now had their original choice back in place. An interesting point to note is that Melora never filmed any scenes with Eric Stoltz, nor later with Michael J. Fox. Bob Gale has stated multiple times in the past that firing Melora because she was too tall was one of the most difficult things he ever did as a producer.

In a 2001 interview with Stephen Clark on BTTF.com, Gale would say, "I'll tell you, it was the hardest thing I ever had to do, breaking the news to Melora, because she didn't do anything to warrant being let go. She was in tears, of course, and I was sick about it for days. I haven't spoken with her in about ten years, but now that I'm thinking about her, I just might have to do that."

That interview would later inspire a comic book called *Back to Back to the Future* by David Guy Levy in which Hardin and Gale travel back in time as themselves and ensure that both Eric Stoltz and Melora Hardin stay on the film. In November of 2013, Gale met Melora for lunch to apologize for having to let her go from *Back to the Future*.

As filming resumed with Fox, the production team faced an immense challenge: they needed to reshoot nearly five weeks' worth of footage previously shot with Stoltz, all while keeping up with a tight summer 1985 release schedule. Director Robert Zemeckis and his crew worked at an exhausting pace, often filming around the clock to meet the deadline. Fox's grueling schedule had him filming *Family Ties* during the day and *Back to the Future* at night, catching only a few hours of sleep in between. Despite the pressure, Fox's charisma on screen made it clear that they had made the right choice.

However, there was one more wrinkle to navigate before the film could be completed. Sid Sheinberg, the head of Universal Pictures and a key supporter of the film, had provided important script notes earlier in production. To reiterate, Sid was responsible for changing Professor Brown to Doc Brown and renaming Marty's mother from Meg to Lorraine (in honor of his wife, actress Lorraine Gary). Perhaps his most significant contribution was replacing Doc Brown's pet chimpanzee, Shemp, with a dog that we came to know and love as Einstein. Sheinberg argued that no movie featuring a chimpanzee had ever been a financial success. When Bob Gale pointed out that Clint Eastwood's *Every Which Way but Loose*, which starred a prime ape as Clint's sidekick, had done well, Sheinberg quipped that the film featured an orangutan, not a chimpanzee.

As the release date loomed, Sheinberg sent a memo to Steven Spielberg, Robert Zemeckis, and Bob Gale with a suggestion for a final change. In his note, Sheinberg proposed renaming the movie to *Space Man from Pluto*. He drew inspiration from a small detail in the film—the comic book Sherman Peabody holds, which features the title *Space Zombies from Pluto* on the cover. Sheinberg believed that *Space Man from Pluto* would make the film sound more fun and exciting, and he was confident it would attract a broader audience.

> Although I believe the present draft is terrific and I'm very pleased with the improvements made from the "Columbia" version, I continue to feel that the title leaves something to be desired. There are several reasons why I find the title less than "wonderful," but my primary concern is that it makes the picture appear to be a "genre" film. I believe both the script and hopefully the film deserve a better title.
>
> Now that I have buttered you up, I would suggest considering the title: *Space Man from Pluto*.
>
> **Underpinning these suggestions are the following thoughts:**
>
> **i.** Modify the dialogue on page 35 so that Sherman calls Marty a "space man from Pluto."
>
> **ii.** Change Marty's dialogue on page 7 so that he identifies himself as a "space man from the Planet Pluto," instead of "Darth Vader from Vulcan."

iii. Change the title of the book written by George and referenced on page 130 from *A Match Made in Space* to *Space Man from Pluto.*

Obviously, you get the idea.

I am sure there will be those who argue that the movie will appear to the audience as a cheap, old-fashioned sci-fi flick. Nonsense! I think it's the kind of title that has *heat, originality,* and *projects fun.* Most importantly, it avoids the feeling of a "genre" time-travel movie.

MCA INTEROFFICE MEMORANDUM

Form 2022 (Rev. 5/82)

DATE	October 17, 1984
TO	Mr. Steven Spielberg
FROM	Sid Sheinberg
SUBJECT	Back to the Future Script
COPIES	Bob Zemeckis Bob Gale

Although I believe that the present draft is terrific and I marvel at the improvements that have been made from the "Columbia" version, I continue to believe the title leaves much to be desired. There are a number of reasons why I found the title less than "wonderful," but my primary concern is that it appears to make the picture a genre picture. I think the script (and, hopefully, the film) deserves a better title.

Now that I have buttered you up, I would suggest we consider the title "Space Man From Pluto."

Underpinning these suggestions are the following thoughts:

i. Modify the dialogue on Page 35 so that Sherman calls Marty a "space man from Pluto."

ii. Modify Marty's dialogue on Page 77 so that he identifies himself as a "space man from the Planet Pluto" (instead of "Darth Vader from Vulcan").

iii. Change the title of the book written by George and referred to on Page 130 from "A Match Made in Space" to "Space Man From Pluto."

Obviously, you get the idea.

I am sure there will be those who argue that the movie will appear to the audience to be a cheap, old-fashioned sci-fi flick. Nonsense! I think it's a kind of title that has heat, originality, and projects fun. Most importantly, I think it avoids the feeling of a genre time-travel movie.

SJS:sl

*recreation of original memo

Spielberg, Zemeckis, and Gale were all floored by the suggestion that *Space Man from Pluto* was a better title than *Back to the Future.* When the two Bobs asked Steven what should be done about this major note from the studio head, Spielberg, always clever with his approach, knew exactly how to handle it. Instead of outright rejecting the idea, Spielberg sent a memo back to Sheinberg, thanking him for his "wonderful joke" and complimenting his sense of humor. The production never heard another word from Sheinberg about the title. As history would prove, Spielberg's tactful response saved the film from an entirely different legacy. Imagine what might have been if audiences had flocked to theaters in 1985 to watch a movie called *Space Man from Pluto.*

This wasn't the end of *Space Man from Pluto,* however. In the 2018 film Eli Roth directed, *A House with a Clock in Its Walls,* starring Jack Black, there is a reference to the title that never was. During a scene in the movie when the character Lewis gets off the bus and is met by his uncle, Jonathan Barnavelt, portrayed by Jack Black, the two walk past a movie theater showing a fictional film called, you guessed it: *Space Man from Pluto.* During an interview on my radio show in 2023 when promoting the film *Thanksgiving,* I asked Eli Roth about his decision to include this little Easter egg in his movie and he told me:

> I love *Back to the Future,* and I also loved that I was making a movie for Amblin. So, I did that for Spielberg. I wanted him to see it, you know, doing the movie for his company. And it felt right. It felt right for the time period of the movie...and I wanted to just give a little nod.

Once the film was released on July 3, 1985, movie-going audiences fell in love with the picture. Once the people saw the iconic DeLorean time machine for the first time, it was all she wrote. *Back to the Future* fired on all cylinders due to a great script that paid off when paired with a wonderfully talented and funny cast, a brilliant director overseeing every aspect of the film, and phenomenal music underscoring all of this. The score of the film, composed and conducted by Alan Silvestri—who went on to score the Avengers films in the MCU—captured the essence and spirit of the film with his dynamic and cinematic score. Most movies in the 1980s were being scored by what Zemeckis refers to as "the box." Films such as *Beverly Hills Cop* or *Fletch* had scores that were electronic and echoed the era, but Zemeckis wanted his time-travel film to have an epic feel to it, exactly what Silvestri brought to the project.

To inject a little bit of rock 'n' roll into *Back to the Future*, Huey Lewis and the News were brought on board to write two songs for the film. At the time, Huey Lewis was a huge name in the music industry, known for his energetic blend of rock and pop that perfectly captured the spirit of the 1980s. The band's 1983 album *Sports* was a massive success, producing hit singles like "Heart and Soul," "I Want a New Drug," and "If This Is It," all of which dominated the airwaves and established the group as one of the era's defining acts.

For *Back to the Future*, Huey Lewis and the News wrote "The Power of Love" and "Back in Time," both of which worked seamlessly within the context of the story. "The Power of Love" became an iconic anthem, not only for the film but for the 1980s. It soared to number one on the Billboard Hot 100 and earned the band an Academy Award nomination for Best Original Song.

Huey Lewis also made a memorable cameo in the film, playing a humorless judge at Marty's high school battle of the bands audition. As Marty's band, The Pinheads, cranked out their electrifying rendition of "The Power of Love," Lewis' character famously shuts them down by declaring, "I'm afraid you're just too darn loud." It was a perfect tongue-in-cheek moment, given that the song Lewis was rejecting was his own hit.

The inclusion of Huey Lewis in the film further cemented his cultural influence in 1985, a year that was a defining moment for him. In addition to his contributions to *Back to the Future*, Lewis was also one of the many stars to participate in the historic recording of "We Are the World," a charity single that brought together the biggest names in music to raise funds for famine relief in Africa. The song, spearheaded by Michael Jackson and Lionel Richie, became a global phenomenon, topping charts around the world and raising millions of dollars.

Around the time of the film's release, Michael J. Fox was in London filming *Family Ties*. Despite the distance, Fox vividly remembers doing interviews with media outlets back in the United States and feeling the mounting excitement and enthusiasm surrounding *Back to the Future*. One memory stands out—receiving a call from his agents informing him that *Back to the Future* was the biggest movie in America and would soon be the biggest movie in the world. The film dominated the box office, holding the number one spot for an incredible eleven out of twelve weeks during that summer of 1985. It was, without a doubt, a monumental success both critically and commercially.

The idea for the film, born from Bob Gale's curiosity about his father's high school yearbook, had blossomed into a global phenomenon, grossing an astonishing $381,109,762 during its original release. The combination of financial success and the worldwide love for the film naturally sparked conversations about a potential sequel. Producer Frank Marshall, along with the rest of the team, began contemplating the possibilities.

In the 1980s, however, the idea of creating franchises wasn't as prevalent as it is today. Studios didn't automatically plan for trilogies or multi-film series, and actors weren't routinely signed on for multiple sequels. When *Back to the Future* first hit theaters, there was no serious consideration for a follow-up film. In fact, Bob Gale has repeatedly stated in interviews that the ending of the movie—where Doc Brown dramatically arrives in the DeLorean, urging Marty and Jennifer to come with him because "something's got to be done about your kids"—was meant as a joke. It was just a fun and exciting way to close the film on a high note, not a setup for a sequel.

However, what the filmmakers didn't realize at the time was that *Back to the Future* had already captured the imaginations of millions. As the DeLorean soared into the sky, leaving fiery tracks behind, the seeds for a sequel were unknowingly planted. The audience, captivated by the idea of time travel, the flying car, and the lovable characters, was eager for more. Once the DeLorean hit eighty-eight miles per hour and disappeared into the future, the next film had, in essence, already begun writing itself.

The world simply wasn't ready to say goodbye to Hill Valley just yet.

LETTERS FROM YOUR FRIENDS IN TIME: CHRIS VAN VLIET

Emmy Award-Winning TV Host, Film Critic, and Podcaster

I'll never forget the first time I saw *Back to the Future*. I was just eight years old and had never seen anything quite like it! How could you not be drawn to Doc Brown's crazy antics? Or fall in love with Marty's relatable charm? Or be seething with anger every time Biff came on the screen?

Even at my young age, I knew that there was so much more to this movie than just a time-traveling DeLorean. Sure, Robert Zemeckis and Bob Gale had written an incredible script. And yes, the movie was cast perfectly. And of course, I was humming Alan Sylvestri's score for weeks. But beyond that was a bigger message—a reminder of how there are truly no accidents in life.

We have all heard the cliché phrase that everything happens for a reason, but *Back to the Future* taught me an even more important lesson: moments matter.

Just think of all the things that have to happen during the 1955 timeline in order for Marty's parents, George and Lorraine, to meet, fall in love, and have a family. It's a series of very specific events that all lead one into another. George falling out of the tree, getting hit by Lorraine's dad, asking her to the Enchantment Under the Sea dance, punching Biff, and the list goes on and on and on.

As *Back to the Future* demonstrates, if just *one* of those events does not happen, then the entire timeline is thrown off and Marty and his siblings never exist. This is heavy!

Now, think about that in your own life. It's something I remind myself of on a daily basis.

What if I floored it through that yellow light instead of stopping? What if I hurried to make the elevator instead of waiting for the next one? What if I didn't pause to hold the door for the person behind me? Every single one of those actions and the consequences that came from them (whether known or unknown) has led to the exact person that I am right now.

One of the biggest examples of this is how I met my wife, Rachel. We met on Hinge, an online dating app. In case you are unfamiliar with how it works, the app shows you other single people in your area based on the criteria you select. One of those categories is how far away they live. When we met, Rachel and I lived exactly forty-three miles from each other. The funny thing is, she set her parameters on the app to only show people within a thirty-mile radius. On the day that we matched, I just so happened to be visiting a friend I hadn't seen in a while who lived a little closer to where Rachel lived. And look at us now—happily married with two kids.

You could call it fate. You could call it being in the right place at the right time. Or maybe, you could be like George McFly and call it your "density"...sorry, I mean destiny.

It's a pleasant reminder that all of those moments that make up your day matter.

To quote our friend Doc Brown: "Your future hasn't been written yet. No one's has. Your future is whatever you make it. So, make it a good one!"

Your Friend in Time,
Chris Van Vliet

CHAPTER 3

LIGHTNING STRIKES TWICE

After the massive success of the first *Back to the Future* film, the studio wasted no time in approaching Bob Gale and Robert Zemeckis to see if they would sign on to create a sequel. It was, after all, the biggest movie of 1985, and the demand for more was undeniable. Gale and Zemeckis agreed to return, but with one condition: Michael J. Fox and Christopher Lloyd had to reprise their iconic roles as Marty McFly and Doc Brown. The two creators believed that without their lead actors, they couldn't tell the kind of story they envisioned. Fortunately, both Fox and Lloyd were on board, but only on the condition that the Bobs—Gale and Zemeckis—were involved. With that mutual agreement, the journey to make a sequel officially began.

The filmmakers set out to see which other actors from the original film would return for the second installment, which was slated for a 1989 release. When they approached Lea Thompson and Thomas F. Wilson, both actors echoed Fox and Lloyd's sentiments: if the Bobs were involved, so were they. However, when it came to Crispin Glover, who had portrayed George McFly in the first film, negotiations hit a snag. Various documentaries and interviews have since revealed differing accounts of why Glover didn't return, ranging from disputes over salary to disagreements about creative direction. Whatever the case, Glover's absence led Gale to make the decision to write George

McFly out of the sequel entirely, stating that in the alternate 1985 (referred to as 1985A), George was dead. For the scenes where George needed to appear, actor Jeffrey Weissman stepped in to play the role, utilizing prosthetics and careful camera angles to avoid drawing too much attention to the recasting.

Another casting change was necessitated by the departure of Claudia Wells, who played Jennifer Parker in the first film. Wells had left the entertainment business to care for her ill mother. After auditions in February 1989 with actresses Julie Warner and Lori Loughlin, the role of Jennifer was recast with Elisabeth Shue, who had recently gained fame for her work in *Adventures in Babysitting, The Karate Kid,* and *Cocktail*. With the core cast now in place, Gale and Zemeckis could begin fleshing out their script for *Back to the Future Part II*.

Initially, the sequel was set to venture into new territory by taking Marty to the 1960s, where Lorraine would be portrayed as a flower child protesting the Vietnam War. The story would involve the future as we saw in the film itself but would feature things such as a 3D holographic concert of Huey Lewis titled "Back to the 20th Century," Marty and Doc escaping police choppers and grenade launchers to get out of the alternate 1985, with an ending of the script which closely mirrors the conclusion of *Back to the Future Part I*, with Doc Brown returning to yell Marty's name. However, instead of setting up another adventure, Doc simply tells Marty that he left his driver's license and some other belongings in the glove compartment. Relieved, Marty and Jennifer walk off into the future as "When I'm Sixty-Four" by The Beatles plays.

However, while working on *Who Framed Roger Rabbit*, Zemeckis had a different idea. He proposed using the time machine to revisit the events of the first film but from a new perspective, allowing the characters to interact with the timeline in fresh and unexpected ways.

Robert Zemeckis reflected on the unique opportunity *Back to the Future Part II* presented him as a filmmaker during an interview on the *Back to the Future* DVD extras:

> I think the second *Back to the Future*, it might be the most interesting movie I ever made. It was a once in a lifetime situation that no other filmmaker has ever had before because here I had a situation where I was doing a sequel to a time-travel movie where a character goes back and visits the original movie, so you have a chance to make the first movie again from another point of view. And it was really something that thrilled me to do it.

Zemeckis added another layer to the story: they could also go back to the Wild West for the final act, turning the film into a mix of sci-fi and classic western—a genre both filmmakers were passionate about. After Gale went to their draft and added in the western aspect of the story, it clocked in at a whopping 230 pages—double the pages in a typical screenplay. The length of the script gave the studio pause, so the *Back to the Future* filmmakers reached an agreement to split the script into two films. Originally, the studio wanted the Bobs to scale down the script because they did not want to release a four-hour, $80 million sequel, and the Bobs did not want to cut out any material. Convincing Universal to allow them to shoot this version of the script as two two-hour sequels with $40 million budgets each was an easier sell, and they didn't have to drop any ideas from their script. The two films were then scheduled to be shot over the course of eleven months. Inspired by Richard Lester's *The Three Musketeers* and *The Four Musketeers*, which had been filmed back-to-back, Gale and Zemeckis embraced the idea. Now, instead of one massive follow-up, the world would get two more *Back to the Future* adventures, exploring even more dimensions of time and character.

The task ahead was immense, but the filmmakers were up for the challenge. What had begun as an effort to satisfy audience demand for a sequel was now something much bigger—a chance to dive deeper into the world they had created and bring Marty and Doc on their most ambitious adventure yet. The sequels began production under the working title *Paradox*, a deliberate attempt to keep prying eyes, the press, and spectators from discovering any details about the highly anticipated future of *Back to the Future*.

The first night of filming *Back to the Future Part II* took place on February 24, 1989, and excitement buzzed in the air as the cast and crew gathered in front of the iconic Hill Valley clock tower. However, while the anticipation was palpable, Christopher Lloyd later revealed that this was one of the toughest nights of his entire experience filming the trilogy. The challenge lay in having to replicate the scene from the end of the original film, but now, four years later, he had to match his performance exactly. This made the process both physically and mentally demanding.

Michael J. Fox arrived on set later that night, coming straight from the Paramount lot after taping *Family Ties*, which was still airing at the time. This mirrored his experience during the filming of the first movie, where he had to juggle his sitcom duties with the demands of filming *Back to the Future*. Ironically, that same night, Fox and Lloyd filmed the final scene of *Back to the Future Part II*.

One of the most complex parts of *Part II* involved revisiting the 1955 scenes from the first film. The crew had to painstakingly recreate the sets on the Universal backlot, ensuring every detail matched the original movie. Integrating the new versions of Marty and Doc into those established scenes required careful planning and innovative camera work, but Zemeckis pulled it off seamlessly.

Many fans of *Back to the Future Part II* were captivated by the 2015 scenes, which showcased incredible future gadgets and technology. These imaginative glimpses into the future became a fan favorite, with audiences continuing to love and revisit them since the film's release. However, during the research for this book, I was surprised to learn that Robert Zemeckis was not fond of the 2015 setting.

In *Back to the Future: The Ultimate Visual History*, Zemeckis reveals that he "always hated" movies about the future and still doesn't enjoy them, explaining, "I just keep thinking they're impossible and somebody's always keeping score." Despite his personal feelings, Zemeckis later reflected that *Back to the Future Part II* may have exceeded everyone's expectations in terms of its futuristic predictions. He acknowledges in the same book, "We're doing pretty good. I think we're batting about 500 on our predictions for the future. We predicted a lot of stuff. So I guess we're kind of futurists. But also, we didn't think of a lot of things." Gale and Zemeckis knew they had to begin *Back to the Future Part II* exactly where the first film left off, with Doc Brown's iconic line, "Roads? Where we're going, we don't need roads." Though creating a believable yet optimistic future was a challenge, especially when most sci-fi films of the era leaned toward dystopian visions, like *Blade Runner*. Zemeckis and his team aimed for something more hopeful.

Even with its imperfections, the 2015 segment of *Back to the Future Part II* remains one of the most beloved portrayals of the future in cinematic history. From Grays Sports Almanac to Pepsi Perfect, Nike Air MAGs, the *Jaws 19* hologram shark, and the Mattel Hoverboard, the filmmakers crafted a vision of the future that was both optimistic and plausible. These futuristic props not only captivated audiences at the time but have since become iconic pieces of pop culture. In fact, the hoverboard generated so much interest that fans clamored for a real-world version, leading to numerous attempts to recreate it.

One of the most notable attempts at recreating the hoverboard came from a company called Hendo, co-founded by Greg and Jill Henderson. Hendo's original goal went beyond just creating a hoverboard for fun—they aimed to develop technology that could use magnetic fields to solve real-world problems. Their vision extended far beyond a cool gadget; they sought to create a system that could potentially lift buildings during floods or earthquakes, shielding them from destruction. This same concept could also be applied as a replacement for the levitation systems currently used in maglev trains.

In 2014, Hendo launched a Kickstarter campaign for their hoverboard, priced at $10,000. While the campaign garnered significant attention, particularly for the board's resemblance to the iconic hoverboard from the film, it still had limitations. Like the fictional hoverboard, Hendo's version relies on magnetic technology, meaning it can only function on specific surfaces—namely, metal. Much like the one in *Back to the Future*, Hendo's board also doesn't work on water.

Despite these limitations, the Hendo hoverboard captured the imagination of many. It drew the attention of *Back to the Future*'s Bob Gale and skateboarding legend Tony Hawk, both of whom visited Hendo's "hover park" to experience this real-life version. While it has yet to hit the mass market, Hendo's innovative work represents one of the closest attempts at bringing the hoverboard fantasy to life.

The final scene of *Part II* set the stage for *Part III*, with Marty receiving a letter from the 1985 Doc Brown, revealing that he had been sent back to 1885 after the DeLorean was struck by lightning. Marty, desperate for help, runs to the 1955 Doc Brown, who promptly faints upon learning that Marty is "back from the future." The film ended with the title card, "to be concluded..." which left audiences eagerly anticipating the final chapter.

Filming for *Back to the Future Part II* spanned nearly twenty-three weeks, wrapping up on August 1, 1989, just three months before the film's release in theaters. As assistant director David McGiffert called out, "That's a wrap!" the cast and crew briefly celebrated the completion of another chapter in the franchise. However, their relief was short-lived—another adventure awaited them 350 miles north in Sonora, California.

Just twenty-eight days after production on *Part II* ended, filming for *Back to the Future Part III* began. Now, shooting six days a week on location, the filmmakers embraced a new challenge—a true western. The core cast returned with exciting new twists: Lea Thompson portrayed Mrs. Margaret McFly, Tom Wilson took on the role of Buford "Mad Dog" Tannen, the great ancestor of Biff, and James Tolkan returned as Marshal James Strickland, overseeing law and order in 1885 Hill Valley. Once again, Michael J. Fox stretched his acting chops, this time portraying Seamus McFly, adding yet another character to his résumé, which already included his older self, his daughter, and his son from *Part II*.

One of the key additions to *Back to the Future Part III* was the casting of Mary Steenburgen as Doc Brown's love interest, Clara Clayton. Steenburgen, already a respected and accomplished actress, brought a new dynamic to the film's narrative by giving Doc Brown a romantic storyline, something that had been absent in the previous installments. Her involvement in the project came after some convincing—not from the filmmakers, but from her children, who were huge fans of the first *Back to the Future* film. They encouraged her to take on the role, and thankfully, she agreed, adding depth to the character of Doc Brown and giving the film an emotional core that resonated with audiences.

Steenburgen wasn't entirely unfamiliar with working alongside Christopher Lloyd, having previously shared the screen with him in the western *Goin' South*, directed by Jack Nicholson. Their previous collaboration added a layer of familiarity and chemistry that carried over into *Part III*, making their on-screen romance feel natural and authentic. Steenburgen's portrayal of Clara brought warmth and tenderness to the film, complementing Doc Brown's eccentricity.

This pairing of Doc and Clara added a new, heartfelt element to the final installment of the trilogy. Clara's character was not just a love interest but also a catalyst for Doc's internal conflict—whether to stay in the past and build a life with her or return to the future with Marty. In many ways, her presence humanized Doc Brown, giving him a personal stake in the narrative and showing a side of him we hadn't seen before.

Throughout the scenes set in 1885 Hill Valley, Marty McFly humorously gives himself the nickname "Clint Eastwood." When Buford "Mad Dog" Tannen hears this, he scoffs, "What kind of stupid name is that?" This was, of course, a nod to the real Clint Eastwood, who by then was a massive star in Hollywood, known for his iconic roles in westerns, particularly the famous Sergio Leone "spaghetti western" trilogy: *A Fistful of Dollars, For a Few Dollars More,* and *The Good, the Bad, and the Ugly.*

But this wasn't the first time Clint Eastwood was referenced in *Back to the Future*. Footage from *A Fistful of Dollars* was shown in *Back to the Future Part II* in Biff's residence, where Biff, let's just say, was "hosting" some company. That scene gave Marty the idea to use a bulletproof vest in *Back to the Future Part III* to trick Buford during their climactic showdown.

However, there's even more to the Eastwood connection. While *A Fistful of Dollars* played its part in the film's story, there's a second reference tied to Marty's joke. In the 1955 drive-in scene, as Marty prepares to travel to 1885, he looks at his outfit and says, "Clint Eastwood never wore anything like this!" As he gestures and walks toward Doc, two posters are visible on the drive-in wall: one for *Revenge of the Creature* and another for *Tarantula!*. Both films featured a young Clint Eastwood, with *Revenge of the Creature* marking his first film role.

The film also featured some familiar faces from classic westerns. Veteran actors like Doug Taylor, Harry Carey Jr., Matt Clark, and Pat Buttram appeared in saloon scenes, lending a layer of authenticity to the western setting. Burton Gilliam, another seasoned actor who made a name for himself in *Fletch* and *Paper Moon*, also made an appearance. In a conversation on my podcast, Gilliam fondly recalled his experience working on the set of *Back to the Future Part III*, reminiscing about the production and how his involvement came to be.

> **BRAD:** You're the Colt Peacemaker salesman in the Old West, and you show Marty McFly the gun and ask him where he learned to shoot like that. How did you get the role in *Back to the Future* [*Part III*]?
>
> **BURTON:** Michael J. Fox wanted me... I didn't know Michael personally, but he knew of me through...the work I had done. He thought it was a good idea. So, they got a hold of my agent, and I didn't have to audition or anything. We just went straight to the set, and I was on the movie for three weeks, even though I only worked two nights.
>
> **BRAD:** That's incredible!

> **BURTON:** Yeah! We shot up in Sonora, California. I think it must've been January or February because it was cold! You see us all at this big square dance party, and we were freezing to death. But we made it look like it was a comfortable evening out there! Trust me, it wasn't—it was a real cold shoot for both nights. But I was on set for three weeks and had a fantastic time. I even got to see *Slim Pickens*, who lived about seven miles away. Every day I had off, I'd be running around with those guys—it was just a good time being up there. And Michael J. Fox, well, he's always been a wonderful friend to me.

Similar to the first installment of the franchise that featured Huey Lewis on the soundtrack and in a cameo, *Back to the Future Part III* followed suit with another iconic musical moment. In the scene where Doc and Clara are dancing before being interrupted by Mad Dog Tannen, the sounds they are grooving to during their rhythmic ceremonial ritual were laid down by the legendary Texas rock band ZZ Top. Billy Gibbons, Dusty Hill, and Frank Beard—known for churning out massive hits like "La Grange," "Sharp Dressed Man," and "Cheap Sunglasses"—lent their musical talents to the film.

In an interview with *Unlimited Classic Rock*, ZZ Top bassist Dusty Hill recalls that it took his persuasion to get the band involved in the movie:

> We got asked, somehow, to write a song to be in the movie called *Doubleback*. Well, we stopped by the set one night. I can't remember where it was, somewhere out in California. They built a whole damn western town. It was really cool. Anyway, they were doing all-night shooting, so we stopped by at midnight or one a.m., and they were shooting this scene. They broke for lunch and I remember that I made sure I was sitting over there by Robert Zemeckis, the director. I kept saying, "You know, it looks

> like we belong in this movie! I mean, you don't hardly even need to use makeup on us!"

Hill's persistence paid off. According to the legendary rocker, Zemeckis was on board with the idea, but a slight adjustment was needed to fit ZZ Top into the film while still winking at the audience.

> They already had a band, so they just added the three of us. To get it where Frank's drum would spin like the guitars did in "Legs" was funny. It turned out to be great. I've got a *Back to the Future* pinball machine that's got the song in it. Anyway, it was fun. I love movies, and I'm interested in watching how they're made and everything.

For *Back to the Future Part III*, producer Kathleen Kennedy highlighted how the time travel element allowed the filmmakers to explore different genres. The first film was a sci-fi adventure, the second had a more action-oriented feel, and the third was a full-fledged western. During filming, Zemeckis discovered why directors loved making westerns. The shoot felt like summer camp—peaceful and quiet, far removed from the hectic pace of city life. Michael J. Fox also embraced the genre, taking advantage of the downtime to fish and enjoy the outdoors. He learned to ride horses and even worked with a quick-draw expert to hone his skills for the film. Gale, too, found *Part III* the most fun to make, as he had always had a deep love for westerns since childhood.

While some fans see *Back to the Future Part III* as a departure from the essence of the original film, others appreciate it as a fun and fitting conclusion to the trilogy. Although it was the least profitable of the three films, it holds a special place in the hearts of the cast and crew, who fondly remember the peaceful and joyous experience of working on the project.

I sometimes think *Back to the Future Part III* is the strongest film in the trilogy. Perhaps it's because I'm from Texas and have a soft spot for westerns, but something about the film's charm and adventure resonates with me. That said, my ranking of the films often fluctuates. During my time hosting *Back to the Future: The Podcast*, I've spoken to many fans who love *Part III* the most, only to later shift their preference to the first or second film.

One person who shares my love for *Back to the Future Part III* is Christopher Lloyd. On March 11, 2021, I had the privilege of speaking with the actor who brought Doc Brown to life while he was promoting *Expedition: Back to the Future* for Discovery+. During our conversation, I told him, "When *Back to the Future Part III* was a western, I absolutely loved that. For the longest time, it was my favorite of the three films. I have to ask you—did you enjoy working on *Back to the Future Part III*, being in that western setting? I actually saw another movie you did, *Goin' South*, which was also a western with Jack Nicholson. Did you enjoy the western motif? And, which of the three films is your personal favorite?"

Christopher responded enthusiastically, saying: "Well, that happens to be my personal favorite."

I couldn't help but laugh and reply, "Look at that!"

He continued: "Yeah. I just grew up with the western mystique in my head. I went to a ranch for a summer in Wyoming and did all the western stuff. I have a kind of affinity for that, so I loved it. I loved it.

Horseback riding, Doc has a romance, I mean, you know? It's just, it's good."

But Christopher Lloyd and I weren't the only ones who shared a mutual love for *Back to the Future Part III*. During an interview with the Fox affiliate in Washington, DC, interviewer Kevin McCarthy asked Academy Award nominee Colin Farrell which movie he had seen the most. Without hesitation, Farrell responded, "Probably *Back to the Future*." McCarthy, excited by the answer, then brought up what he said was a big debate among his friends, saying, "I love *[Part] III*, but *[Part] I* is obviously the classic." To this, Farrell enthusiastically responded, "I love three, three is tons of fun. I love them all!"

It's clear that even Farrell shares an appreciation for the Wild West adventure that often gets overlooked in favor of the original, but still holds a special place for many fans, myself included.

During the production of *Back to the Future Parts II* and *III*, Michael J. Fox underwent a profound personal transformation. He concluded his long-running role as Alex P. Keaton on *Family Ties*, which had been a defining part of his career. During this transition, Fox and his wife, actress Tracy Pollan, welcomed their first child. At the same time, he faced the emotional toll of losing his father, adding another layer of complexity to an already challenging period in his life.

All of these personal milestones unfolded while Fox was navigating the intense schedule of filming two *Back to the Future* sequels back-to-back. The demanding nature of the production—often requiring him to balance different timelines and character developments—was physically and mentally exhausting. However, this period also became a defining one for Fox, both professionally and personally, as it tested his resilience and adaptability, ultimately shaping the trajectory of his life and career.

One thing is undeniable: the *Back to the Future* trilogy has earned its place as one of the greatest film trilogies ever made. Its influence spans across generations, captivating audiences with its perfect blend of heart, humor, and adventure. The visionaries behind it all—Bob Gale and Robert Zemeckis—deserve endless gratitude for giving us this unforgettable time travel saga. They created a cinematic world so rich and detailed that it has become a cultural touchstone, referenced and revered decades after its original release.

LETTERS FROM YOUR FRIENDS IN TIME: JEFF SMITH

Director of *Who Done It: The Clue Documentary*

I am a man of many passions. Movies, theme parks...okay, just two passions. And both of these passions began in my childhood.

As a kid of the '80s, certain TV shows were simply required viewing, and *Family Ties* was one of them. It was a Wednesday night staple (until it moved to Thursdays in 1987 and then Sundays in 1989). So, when I heard that my hero, Michael J. Fox, was starring in a new movie in the summer of 1985, I knew I'd be begging my family to take me. That film, of course, was *Teen Wolf*. But before Michael J. Fox transformed into a werewolf ("Geez, Louise"), he was already diving head-first into a DeLorean to take a trip to 1955 in *Back to the Future*. To say I enjoyed the film would be an understatement.

Living in Southern California, there were several theme parks within an hour or two of my house. I lived much closer to Disneyland and Knott's

Berry Farm but every year on my birthday, my family and I would take the treacherous journey through LA traffic to visit the original Universal Studios. And in the summer of '85, when we all got in line for the world-famous Studio Tour to see the flash flood and the parting of the Red Sea, my jaw dropped when I saw *that* car! It was Doc Brown's time machine parked right there in the queue. *Back to the Future* wasn't just a hit in movie theaters—it became part of the Universal Parks experience. Even today, the Studio Tour still passes through Hill Valley town square, complete with the iconic clock tower.

Back to the Future even played a role in bringing us Universal Studios Florida. In 1986, when George Lucas was developing the "Star Tours" attraction for Disneyland, he invited Steven Spielberg (the executive producer of *Back to the Future*) to check it out. Lucas famously told Spielberg that only Disney could create such a ride. Spielberg replied, "We'll just see about that, sucka!" (I'm paraphrasing, of course). This challenge inspired Spielberg to get on his pals at Universal to create something just as cool as "Star Tours." That idea not only resulted in plans for Back to the Future: The Ride, but this concept helped jumpstart Universal's plans for a Florida theme park.

In 1991, my family and I flew to Universal Studios Florida, and I got to experience Back to the Future: The Ride for the first time. It was the closest we ever got to a fourth film. The ride featured Christopher Lloyd as Doc Brown and Thomas F. Wilson as Biff Tannen. This attraction recruited riders to stop Biff from stealing Doc's time machine. We zoomed through the future (Hill Valley 2015), got swallowed by a dinosaur, and returned to the present day at Doc Brown's Institute of Future Technology. And Biff called us "buttheads." Vacation complete.

While I'll always remember seeing all three *Back to the Future* films in theaters, I'll also never forget "riding the movies" at Universal Studios

Hollywood and Florida. Fans like me, who were in awe of Michael J. Fox racing down Hill Valley's main street at eighty-eight miles per hour, got the chance to visit the "real" town and sit in the driver's seat of a DeLorean ourselves. It was pretty heavy.

Your Friend in Time,
Jeff Smith

PART II

TO BE CONTINUED

CHAPTER 4

THE INSTITUTE OF FUTURE TECHNOLOGY

For as long as I can remember, I have loved theme parks. To this day, I find myself listening to podcasts such as *Podcast: The Ride*, watching YouTube channels like "Defunctland" and "Theme Park History," and being awe-inspired by documentaries such as the docuseries *The Imagineering Story* by Leslie Iwerks on Disney+. It all started when I was young. My father worked for a telecommunications company with Buena Vista (a subsidiary of the Walt Disney Company at the time) as a client. This allowed many perks for my family, including three trips to Walt Disney World in Orlando, Florida, in a single year. The VIP experience at Disney World is too much for any child to handle. I rode Pirates of the Caribbean, The Haunted Mansion, Splash Mountain, and others seemingly dozens of times before my tenth birthday. The house that Mickey built was ingrained in my DNA from that age on, and now working under Disney's ESPN banner, I am even more of a Mickey Mouse guy than ever before.

Even though my mouse ears were seemingly sewn onto my head, never to come off, I have my eye on one attraction outside of a Disney park. Universal Studios had the one ride I wanted to experience more than any other. In 2004, I graduated from elementary school and was onto junior high, and during that summer I had one goal in mind: ride the Back to the Future: The Ride at Universal Studios before the beginning of the sixth grade. When I floated this potential travel plan to my parents, they were not particularly warm to the idea of going on a summer vacation just because I felt accomplished for completing the fifth grade.

After failing in my attempt to go to Orlando that summer, I hatched my plan. I went to my sister Brittney, who is almost seven years older than me, and asked her (if I had saved enough money) whether she would take me to Universal upon my eighth-grade graduation. After she kind of shrugged it off as a future favor too far in advance to consider, she agreed. I began to save my money over the next three years, and I think the box of change that I accrued would have been just enough to finally achieve the goal of riding what many people considered the fourth installment of the franchise.

When I walked across the stage at Lanier Middle School, I went to my sister to see if our plans were still intact. After my inquiry, she seemed not to remember what I was talking about. Right around the time of my graduation, she worked full-time at a brand-new job and was attending university, so she may have been a tad busy to take her little brother nearly one thousand miles to go to a theme park. I gave up on my goal for the time being and thought I might go on my own after I turned eighteen. Well, four months later, Back to the Future: The Ride closed in Orlando for good.

Almost immediately after *Back to the Future* was released in 1985, people wanted more of the time-traveling tale. Universal Studios, the production studio behind *Back to the Future* and its eventual sequels, was also in development of something for its own future. The movie studio had its eyes set on Orlando, Florida, as they wanted to compete in the theme park market with Walt Disney World on the East Coast. The park would eventually come to fruition in 1990 and was dubbed

Universal Studios Orlando, and they had quite the ace up their sleeve to help with the creative decisions of the park. Steven Spielberg was hired as a creative consultant for the new park, and he assisted with developing attractions for Universal Studios Hollywood. In 1986, during a meeting between Spielberg and Peter Alexander, a Universal Studios creative executive, the two men discussed possible attractions to compete with Disneyland's Star Tours, which Spielberg had recently ridden due to his friendship with *Star Wars* creator George Lucas. When Lucas told Steven that "Universal could never do a Star Tours," Spielberg told Alexander that they should begin coming up with ideas based on *Back to the Future* to combat the leader of the *Star Wars* Empire's statement.

In 1988, the executives of Universal Parks gave the green light to begin working on the attraction. In the initial planning stages of the ride, the idea was to make an eighteen-passenger DeLorean roller coaster. Although this idea is awesome, a fast-paced rollercoaster that could get close to the eighty-eight mph needed to "travel through time" was scrapped due to worries that the ride would be too fast to tell an effective story. The designers of the attraction came up with the idea to take what Star Tours did and improve it. With the idea of making the ride a simulation experience, the design team laid out what would eventually become one of the most beloved attractions in theme park history. The team came up with the idea of projecting a film on an eighty-foot dome-shaped OMNIMAX® screen. Inside, guests would ride vehicles resembling the DeLorean, which would move in time to the film.

Universal knew that the production of the ride film needed to match the thrill and excitement of its 1985 predecessor as much as possible. To take on the job of creating the film, Universal enlisted Greg MacGillivray. MacGillivray would eventually be nominated for an Academy Award in 1995 and in 2000 for his work on the documentaries *The Living Sea* and *Dolphins*. He was hired mainly for his extensive knowledge of and experience with the IMAX camera format. MacGillivray was teamed with talented special effects artist Richard Edlund.

To match the awe the audience felt when they walked out of theaters in the summer of 1985, Universal thought that Edlund would be a great choice for the job. Edlund was a special effects wizard who worked on *Star Wars*, *The Empire Strikes Back*, *Raiders of the Lost Ark*, *Ghostbusters*, *Die Hard*, and *The Hunt for Red October*. That kind of film career, most of which he had done prior to his enlistment with Universal, would lead one to believe he could get the proverbial "job done" along with MacGillivray.

MacGillivray and Edlund began crafting their version of time-traveling cinema and put together a demo reel of their work thus far. MacGillivray had an idea true to the roots of Universal Studios' initial concept of "riding the movies." From my research, MacGillivray wanted to make the attraction a fly-over experience with park-goers seeing Hill Valley and familiar events from the franchise from above. According to *Back to the Future: The Ultimate Visual History*, Bob Gale, who was not involved in the creation of the ride as was the case with Robert Zemeckis, said the demo footage he saw was "absolutely terrible" and "just bad."

Obviously, this was not the reaction Universal was looking for. Universal had to decide to either continue with the team of MacGillivray and Edlund or move the project in a different direction, leaving Back to the Future: The Ride's future in jeopardy. The project did move forward, but not with its previous team. Universal made the decision to give someone new a crack at crafting the future and called Douglas Trumbull.

The last thing Douglas Trumbull was expecting was a call from Sherry McKenna, a Universal Studios producer, asking for his help to get the *Back to the Future* project back on track. Trumbull, who was a visual effects artist and worked on films such as *Bladerunner*, had prior knowledge and experience working with simulator rides. After viewing the footage MacGillivray and Edlund had produced, Trumbull decided to move in a different direction. Trumbull's idea was for parkgoers to board a DeLorean and fly through time while visiting Hill Valley's landmarks throughout the years. The fly-over experience sought to make the riders of the attraction part of the story rather than a spectator as in an attraction like Pirates of the Caribbean. Trumbull's ideas were met with enthusiasm, and he was hired for the job.

While the production of the ride system itself was underway under Trumbull's watch, the concept of the story was still not fully fleshed out. At one point, the story would feature two Doc Browns. Now, after watching *Back to the Future*, one would understand that having two of the same character at the same time would not be too unusual. But the studio wasn't thinking four-dimensionally—more in terms of a low-budget soap opera. The idea of the two Doc Browns would be the Doc Brown you knew and loved from the movies, and the other Doc Brown would be his evil twin brother. According to Peyton Reed in an interview conducted by Stephen Clark circa 1995, Doc Brown's evil twin brother was supposed to be named "Stan Brown"—also to be portrayed by Christopher Lloyd. Yeah, that almost happened. But thankfully, the team working on the Back to the Future: The Ride brought in the perfect person to nail down the story.

A young aspiring filmmaker named Peyton Reed was hired to create and construct the ride's all-important preshow film and overall narrative. Reed and his partner Mark Cowen helped create an entertaining storyline that fans would appreciate. Reed thought that the two Doc Browns concept was silly and would not be received well by fans of the trilogy. Reed and Cowen thought that the perfect antagonist for the preshow and ride was the same villain from the movies, Biff Tannen. Reed and Cowen pitched the idea that Biff would steal the DeLorean time machine and then would be chased through all the different time periods of Hill Valley.

After several years of development, the ride officially opened in Universal Studios Florida in May of 1991 with its counterpart in Hollywood coming out about twenty-five months later. The grand premiere with the worldwide press, attended by Michael J. Fox, Tom Wilson, and Mary Steenburgen, took place on May 1, 1991. The attraction officially opened the next day on May 2, 1991. Fans from all over the world visited the attraction at Universal Studios Florida, and the ride was touted as one of the best rides ever created. This was especially impressive for Universal, which had been responsible for some theme park blunders; most notably, the *Jaws* ride that had many technical issues, which led to a passenger falling off the boat and sustaining injuries resulting in a lawsuit and a closure of the attraction less than ninety days after its opening. None of these issues were present in the Back to the Future: The Ride; the ride was a success that took visitors through an experiment in time by our faithful Dr. Brown.

The preshow film opens with a message from Heather, who works as a receptionist at the Institute of Future Technology. Heather was portrayed by actress Darlene Vogel, who also played the character Spike, a member of Griff Tannen's gang, in *Back to the Future Part II*. Heather wishes the viewers a pleasant visit to the institute, which was founded by Dr. Emmett Brown. A logo for the institute flashes on the screen and then we are taken to a video package documenting the series of events that led to Dr. Brown inventing the time machine in 1985 and then the time machine's evolutions over the three films.

Then a voiceover states that a sub-ether transmission from 2015 was incoming, and after a flash of the screen, we see Doc in the flying DeLorean time machine driving on the Hill Valley skyway. After almost being hit by a car, Doc explains that the viewers of the film are to be volunteers in a science experiment that will send everyone one day into the future.

The only problem is the "whenabouts" of Biff Tannen are unknown. The fact that Biff could be gallivanting through the space-time continuum could skew history as we know it, so Doc seems more in crisis than normal.

We then are shown a segment called "Doc on the March," where we see Doc Brown through time meeting other great inventors such as himself. Doc is shown chatting it up with Edison, watching the Wright Brothers' first flight, posing for pictures with Albert Einstein, standing behind President Nixon for a speech, and finally taking photos of The Beatles during their first trip to America. All of these segments were done with real archival footage of these events with Doc green-screened into them. The "Doc on the March" segment has drawn comparisons to another Zemeckis film, *Forrest Gump*, which featured similar techniques of splicing historical footage and figures in with its fictional lead character.

Doc then comes back onto the screen from 2015 and informs us that Biff is on the loose and will only use time travel for his benefit, as he did with the sports almanac in *Part II*. Doc says that future information should not be abused, and he even shows a "Zemeckis-Gale Model" to illustrate his point. Another video is played that details more historical background about Doc. The preshow film was made to be long enough to entertain people waiting in the queue for up to forty-five minutes. As Doc returns to the present, he finally welcomes the volunteers of the experiment inside the Institute of Future Technology and shows a couple of inventions they have been working on. One such invention was the "suc-o-matic," a vacuum cleaner powered by the dust it picks up. After a plume of dust blasts Doc in the face, Doc shows us a machine that turns manure into fuel, a mind-reading device based on his 1955 prototype, and the newly designed eight-passenger DeLorean time machine.

Heather returns to the screen as she briefs the volunteers that a security breach has occurred and asks everyone to stand by. The security cameras then show Biff Tannen has broken into the institute, and he attempts to recruit volunteers to help him find the DeLorean. After Biff evades security, he pulls the plug on Doc's laboratory. When the power comes back on in the lab, Doc continues to brief guests on the time travel experiment and does not see Young Biff Tannen from 1955 sneaking up behind him. Biff smashes a couple of buttons with a monkey wrench, and the chain reaction causes jail-like bars to come down from the ceiling, locking Doc out of the portion of the lab where the time machine is housed. It is revealed that Biff stowed away in the time machine during one of the institute's time-travel missions in 1955, which is how Young Biff is now in the present. Biff tells Doc he is going on a joy ride in the time machine, and Doc recruits the volunteers to chase down Biff and prevent him from causing any irreparable damage to the space-time continuum.

The volunteers first catch Biff in 2015 as he causes the eight-passenger DeLorean to crash through the Hill Valley clock tower. Then, it's millions of years into the past during the Ice Age of the future California town. The Ice Age causes a temporary failure of the time machine before it restarts and zooms into the future to the Cretaceous period. The time machine is swallowed and spit up by a Tyrannosaurus Rex, and the two-time vehicles fall into an underground pit full of lava. The flux capacitor of Biff's stolen time machine goes out, and Biff asks Doc for help. Doc remotely accelerates the passengers' ride vehicle up to eighty-eight mph and bumps the time machine Biff was driving, causing both vehicles to return to the present and arrive safely back at the institute.

The ride was enjoyed thousands of times by millions of park-goers for more than a decade. In the mid-2000s, Universal Studios decided it was time to replace the Back to the Future: The Ride with a new intellectual property. The studio decided that *The Simpsons*, the animated family from Springfield, would be the perfect IP to replace Back to the Future: The Ride. The ride officially closed its doors in Hollywood and Florida in 2007, but the version of the ride housed at Universal Studios Japan lasted from 2001 until 2016.

I spoke with Jack, who runs a channel on YouTube called "Theme Park History." Jack, an expert on all things theme parks, compared the Back to the Future: The Ride with its successor. Jack told me that Back to the Future: The Ride was better than The Simpsons Ride.

> *Back to the Future* had more creativity and charm and was seen by many as a "mini-sequel" to the trilogy. The ride was revolutionary when it opened, and it helped motion simulator ride systems be taken seriously. Plus, you got to ride in your very own DeLorean. It's not that The Simpsons Ride isn't a great attraction. It just doesn't capture the magic of what Back to the Future: The Ride inspired.

I kick myself from time to time for not experiencing a ride based on my favorite film franchise of all time. But I hold out hope that Universal Studios will realize that *Back to the Future* means so much to millions of people. I'm not saying that *The Simpsons* doesn't, but *Back to the*

Future is about more than a family that is led by a dopey father as *The Simpsons* is. It's a film about the values of family and how there's nothing more important. That's why Marty McFly finds himself always completing a task to ensure his family's prosperity. For park-goers, many of which are family units, *Back to the Future* is a property that should have a presence in the way of a major attraction for families to enjoy together. Maybe it will be revived sometime in the future.

CHAPTER 5

ANIMATING THE FUTURE

To this day, animation is the dominant form of entertainment for children of all ages. Before the advent of Netflix, Hulu, or YouTube, Saturday morning was for watching large blocks of cartoons. From the late 1980s until today, movie studios looked to profit from big blockbuster films even more by creating animated spin-offs. This led to many questionable series being ordered, including *RoboCop* and *Rambo* animated series based on their R-rated big-screen counterparts and series such as *Men in Black*, *Beetlejuice*, and *Godzilla*, all mainstays in my animation rotation. But I discovered one series as a kid that satiated my time-travel tastebuds.

After the release of *Back to the Future Part III* in 1990, Universal Studios was looking to expand the franchise even further. Famously, the *Back to the Future* creators wore shirts to the *Part III* premiere that read "*Back to the Future IV*" with a circle and a line through it around the Roman numeral part of the logo. This was the not-quite-so-subtle message to the film studio and the fans of the trilogy to not hold their breath for another movie. However, Universal Studios did not relent in their desire for more *Back to the Future*-related content. The studio asked Bob Gale if he would be interested in doing an animated series for *Back to the Future*. Gale agreed to do the project as long as two conditions were met. First, Gale said he needed Christopher Lloyd involved in the project (if he was available). Second, he wanted an educational aspect to the series that would teach young kids about history and science.

The latter request was an idea that came to Bob due to his love of a show called *Watch Mr. Wizard* that Gale watched as a child. *Watch Mr. Wizard* ran from 1951 to 1965 on NBC and featured science experiments that kids could do at home. The show was watched live by millions of people every week and was eventually revived by Nickelodeon in the 1980s and then dubbed *Mr. Wizard's World*. Gale said in "Drawn to the Future," a featurette on the DVD release of the animated series, that one of the reasons he wanted a *Mr. Wizard*-style segment was because his daughter was two years old at the time, and he was concerned by the lack of educational substance of the shows she would watch growing up.

Both of Gale's requests were okayed by the studio, and the series was given the green light for twenty-six episodes of new stories featuring your favorite citizens of Hill Valley, past and present. Gale was then introduced to the man who would write and produce the show with him, John Ludin. Ludin began his career working for the Walt Disney Company. After seeing *The Muppet Movie*, Ludin was determined to work with Jim Henson, the legendary visionary and creator of the Muppets. Ludin pitched two different projects to Henson. Although the two never worked together on Ludin's ideas, Henson and Ludin did keep in touch over the years. Before his work on *Back to the Future: The Animated Series*, Ludin worked on another time travel animated adaptation in 1990, *Bill and Ted's Excellent Adventures*, so he was more than familiar with the genre. Ludin was initially excited to work on the series because of the involvement with Amblin and the opportunity to continue the *Back to the Future* lore, but he quickly realized how daunting the task was. Ludin said in the same "Drawn to the Future" featurette that films were made with a beginning and an end in mind, but a series is completely different because its plot would have to be based on sustaining weekly stories with the same characters. Ludin realized his task was great, but when he saw a Civil War drum that belonged to a relative of his wife, Mary Jo Ludin, who would write episodes for the series, he got an idea for the first episode. Ludin was intrigued by the idea of brothers being on opposing sides of the civil war and thought that having Jules and Verne in this predicament might make for an interesting first show.

Ludin liked the idea of featuring the Doc Brown boys (and their relationship with each other as well as their father) as opposed to Marty, who many people assumed the show would be centered on. Ludin floated this idea to Gale, who loved the concept because Gale felt that kids would be more engaged in seeing other kids their age instead of teenage rockers. Ludin and his team worked on several concepts of what the show should be. After they finally arrived at the best idea, they drafted a script and presented it to Gale.

Gale read the script and immediately threw it in the trash and said that Ludin and his team could do better. Ludin was motivated by this and worked harder on the concept before pitching it to Gale again a month later. Gale loved what they had come up with. The Brown boys were characters not fleshed out in the cinematic trilogy—they were only in one scene and had no dialogue. Gale and Ludin decided that Jules would be a boy virtually like his father, an intellectual who wielded a sharp and vast vocabulary, while Verne was a Dennis the Menace type—a troublemaker and wildcard.

Ludin recalls pitching the concept to another big name, perhaps the biggest name in Hollywood, Steven Spielberg. Being an Amblin show, the concept for *Back to the Future: The Animated Series* would need to be given the once-over by the executive producer of the original trilogy and the head honcho of Amblin Entertainment. When Ludin explained that the series would be a live-action and animated mash-up, Spielberg balked. Then, when Ludin stated they would try to book Christopher Lloyd to reprise his live-action role as Doc Brown, Spielberg replied by saying, "Good luck trying to book him."

After *Back to the Future*'s success, Lloyd was cast in several films such as Uncle Fester in *The Addams Family* and Charlie Wilcox in *Suburban Commando*, both of which were released in 1991 and shot during the preproduction process of the animated series. So, it wasn't unreasonable that Lloyd's schedule could have prevented his involvement in the project. Steven Spielberg gave Ludin one more piece of advice. He told Ludin that he had better make the series "as good as the movies." That was a tall enough task for anyone, but Ludin and Gale were both thrilled when they were indeed able to book Christopher Lloyd for the show. They were confident that his reprisal of Doc Brown would give the show an extra gigawatt or two and accelerate the series to eighty-eight mph.

Unfortunately, Lloyd's schedule would not allow him to voice Doc Brown's animated character. That task was given to Dan Castellaneta, a voice actor you might know as the voice of Homer Simpson in *The Simpsons*. The same was the story with Michael J. Fox, who was not involved in the animated series as he was filming *Doc Hollywood* and *The Hard Way* during this time. But the series producers cast David Kaufman as Marty. Gale and Ludin thought Kaufman did a great job capturing Michael J. Fox's voice as Marty, and Kaufman did so well at voicing Marty that he was cast to play Stuart Little in the animated spin-off of the Michael J. Fox film of the same name in which Fox voiced the titular character. Clara Clayton and Biff Tannen were voiced by the same actors who played them on the big screen, Mary Steenburgen and Thomas F. Wilson, respectively. Rounding out the voice cast was Danny Mann as Einstein, Josh Keaton as Jules Brown, and Troy Davidson as Verne Brown.

With the voice cast now in place, the episodes went into production. Unlike other animated shows at the time that would record each voice actor's dialogue one character at a time, *Back to the Future*'s cast would record them all together. This method led to better fluidity in the scene dialogue and allowed for more energy to be present in the show. Also, the show attempted to refrain from using any real historical figures. Instead, when characters in the series would find themselves in a different time, they would interact with an ancestor of the McFly, Brown, or Tannen families. There was an exception. In one episode titled "Go Fly a Kite," Jules convinces Verne that Doc Brown is not his biological father. While investigating this claim, Verne thinks his real father was one of the founding fathers, Benjamin Franklin. Verne goes to meet Franklin and inadvertently interferes with Franklin's kite experiment where he invents electricity. Aside from that one occurrence, the series kept out of other historical figures' business, to avoid causing a paradox of some kind.

The live-action segment of the *Back to the Future* series turned out to produce major talent. Aside from the incomparable Christopher Lloyd, they featured a relatively unknown assistant named Bill Nye. Nye was a well-educated man who studied at Cornell University in New York. After Nye graduated in 1977 with a degree in mechanical engineering, he worked for the Boeing Corporation for nearly a decade. After pursuing a comedy career beginning in 1978 where Nye won a Steve Martin look-a-like contest, Nye pursued his entertainment career and landed a semi-regular role on the local Seattle sketch comedy show *Almost Live!* After ironically correcting the show's host John Keister's pronunciation of the word "gigawatt,"

Keister responded, "Who do you think you are—Bill Nye the Science Guy?"

To say the least, the name stuck, and the Science Guy was featured on shows such as *Fabulous Wetlands* and Disney Channel's *All-New Mickey Mouse Club*. It wasn't until Bill was cast as Doc Brown's assistant on the animated series that Nye was recognized as a talent who could carry a show on his own. Partly due to his work on *Back to the Future: The Animated Series*, Nye got the chance to host his own show less than a year after the series went off the air. Nye hosted one hundred episodes of *Bill Nye the Science Guy*, and the show's five-year run made him a household name. Nye credits his work with *Back to the Future: The Animated Series* as the reason he got his own show.

I had the pleasure of speaking with Bill Nye on my radio show while he was promoting *The End Is Nye*, and naturally, I had to ask him about his time working on *Back to the Future: The Animated Series*. Nye had a unique role on the show, contributing to the science demonstrations featured between animated segments. Here's what he had to say:

> Oh, it was cool. I didn't have any words. I didn't say anything. I designed most of the demonstrations, but they didn't let me talk. But it was a start. It was a foot in the door; it was a clamp on the test tube. What was it? It was the beginning. So I worked with a guy, John Luden, who's still around and doing that thing, and Christopher Lloyd, the guy who played Doc Brown. Doc Brown would come to the studio and we would do some science demonstrations. It was fun. But that's a niche, man. That's a niche. That's an older show. Lost the reference, lost on many of the younger listeners, but big fun at the start of things. That was a science-based interlude and it was part of the response to the

> Children's Television Act, where you had this entertainment show based on very popular science fiction and then slipped in the middle was a real science lesson.

Peyton Reed also got his start due to the series. Reed's start with *Back to the Future* first began with the 1989 TV special "*Back to the Future Part II* Sneak Peek" hosted by Leslie Nielsen. He then continued with his work on *The Secrets of the Back to the Future Trilogy* and was involved in the theme park ride, working on the live-action preshow film. Reed directed all of the experiments and live-action segments during the first season of the show, writing at least three of the segments himself. If you are reading this and aren't familiar with Peyton Reed, do yourself a solid and scroll through his weighty IMDb page. Reed directed such films as *Bring It On*, which helped launch the careers of Kirsten Dunst and Gabrielle Union; *The Break-Up*, a comedy that starred Vince Vaughn and Jennifer Aniston at the peaks of their careers; and of course 2015's *Ant-Man* and its sequels 2018's *Ant-Man and the Wasp* and 2023's *Ant-Man and the Wasp: Quantumania*, three films from the Marvel Cinematic Universe, the most profitable film franchise in history.

Even with all the talent in the show, the *Back to the Future* animated series did not live past its twenty-six-episode commitment. The show was canceled by CBS for low ratings. However, the show lives on with fans of the trilogy. When I tried to find the show as a young kid, it wasn't readily available. I first learned of the show while watching the twentieth-anniversary collection of the trilogy where it was mentioned by Bob Gale briefly. After searching the internet, I found and immediately purchased a VHS tape of two of the episodes. The tape featured the episodes "Forward to the Past" and "Verne Hatches an Egg." These would be the only episodes of the show I saw for several years. Sometime after the twenty-fifth anniversary of the films, my interest in the animated series was again at an all-time high. After some research, I discovered that eighteen of the twenty-six shows were released on home video in the United States. I took to Twitter and asked my followers if they knew where I could find these episodes. I eventually received a direct message from a user who said they had the series and would send it to me. I gave the person my mailing address, and I was sent a large box full of VHS cassettes that had the original series taped on them. I am not sure where these came from or how the Twitter user got them, but I got to watch the series for the first time as an adult, commercials and all, about seven years after first learning of the series. I loved every episode.

The series isn't talked about enough in the fan community, and many fans do not consider the animated events as canon alongside the original trilogy. Several fun episodes and storylines from the show are a treat to fans of the *Back to the Future* universe. During the run of the series, McDonald's produced four different toys based on the characters in the series for their Happy Meal toys. The four toys featured Doc Brown in the DeLorean time machine, Marty McFly on his hoverboard, Verne Brown in the junk-mobile that was introduced in the episode "A Verne by Any Other Name," and Einstein in the "Jules Verne" time train. The *Back to the Future*-themed toys were introduced in a television commercial that was voiced by Dan Castellaneta. The toys have become collector's items that any true *Back to the Future* fans have in their possession.

The series also gave birth to the first set of comic books based on the franchise. Harvey Comics published seven comic books from 1991 to 1993 featuring our most beloved time travelers. In the first issue of the series, Marty McFly and Doc Brown travel to 1927 Chicago, where prohibition was the law of the land and the mob was in power. Marty and Doc run into Mugsy Tannen and "Bathtub" Jim McFly, and the adventure officially kicks off. The run of the seven comic books came and went as the series did, but the idea of continuing the stories from the travels of Doc and Marty in a comic book was something that Bob Gale saw promise in.

Another notable extension of the *Back to the Future* franchise came in 2010 with *Back to the Future: The Video Game*. Developed by Telltale Games, the game was released in five episodic installments starting in December of 2010 and offered fans a continuation of the beloved storyline. Telltale collaborated closely with the original filmmakers, including Bob Gale, who advised on the narrative, ensuring the game stayed true to the spirit of the films.

Christopher Lloyd reprised his iconic role as Dr. Emmett L. Brown; however, Michael J. Fox did not voice Marty McFly. Instead, the character was voiced by AJ Locascio, whose audition tape impressed the team with his uncanny ability to match Fox's tenor, tone, and inflection. Director of the video game series, Dennis Lenart noted that Tom Wilson, who originally played Biff, was unavailable during the game's production, though they hoped to involve him in the future—a hope that ultimately did not materialize for the original release.

I spoke with AJ Locasio on *Back to the Future: The Podcast* and asked him how he landed the role of voicing one of the most iconic characters in the history of pop culture. AJ shared the surreal experience of how he landed the role of voicing Marty McFly:

> So, I was working in Queens at a therapeutic resource center where they edit videos to educate people on how to deal with kids with autism. It was a sort of detour after college, but it was editing. And so, I was like, cool, I'm using my education to actually work and make money. I had a lot of downtime there, so

> I was browsing the internet and saw that Telltale had announced *Jurassic Park* and *Back to the Future,* and it's weird even talking about this now. I remember the ping of excitement I got seeing that this was going to happen. There was this very surreal feeling like, "How are they going to do that? You can't turn *Back to the Future* into a video game. What is Marty going to do, run around shooting people? How is that possible?" That's insane.

Later that night, as AJ took a train back to New Jersey, he couldn't stop thinking about it.

> I was listening to the *Back to the Future* soundtrack, just sort of obsessing over how cool it was. Somehow, my cousin called me, and he was like, "Did you hear they're turning *Back to the Future* into a game?" And I was like, "Yeah, I did." Then he said, "You should do the voice." I was like, "What do you mean?" And he said, "You should audition for the voice; you should contact them and try to audition."

AJ went home, got on his computer, and contacted Telltale Games.

> I left a message saying, "Hey, my name is AJ, and I do Marty McFly's voice... I'd really like to audition if you don't already have Michael J. Fox lined up. I'd love to be considered as a sound-alike."

To his surprise, within a day or so, he received a response asking for an MP3 of his audition.

> I ran to EB Games and got a rock band mic that I taped to a paint can. My first audition was through that. By the way, that

> rock band mic, I used it for so many auditions. I got my current agent with that mic. It went very far.

After sending in his audition, AJ didn't hear back for months. During that time, he decided New Jersey and New York weren't working out for him anymore, so he made a big life decision.

> I was really depressed, really lost. I had just gone to school for film, and I didn't know what I was doing. Then, my friend said, "Hey, I need a roommate in LA." So I packed up my car, drove across the country, and moved in with my friend.

Just a week after his move, he received another call.

> They said, "Hey, it's between you and one other person. Can you send in another audition?" So I did. But I didn't hear anything back for a little while, and the whole time I was freaking out. I had just moved to a new city, and now I was on the verge of something that could change my life.

The anticipation was overwhelming.

> I couldn't sleep, couldn't eat. I was dreaming about doing something with Christopher Lloyd. There was nothing cool about how I reacted to all this. I was like any other huge *Back to the Future* fan, just obsessing over how incredibly cool this was.

Then, the call came.

> I got it. And I basically turned into a puddle of nothing. I was so overwhelmed. A couple weeks later, they flew me up to do my first session, and it was nuts. It was just nuts.

The game's story picks up on May 14, 1986. Marty McFly is struggling to adapt to life without Doc Brown, whose house is being foreclosed after his mysterious disappearance six months earlier. The opening of the game mirrors a scene familiar to fans, with Doc conducting the temporal experiment, which ultimately leads to his disappearance.

Marty embarks on a time-traveling adventure, landing in 1931, where he encounters Kid Tannen and a young version of Doc. Upon returning to 1986, Marty discovers that Hill Valley has become a dystopian, totalitarian society led by "Citizen Brown." He soon learns that Edna Strickland, a relative of Mr. Strickland, had influenced Doc to abandon science in favor of law, using his intellect to help build her vision of a "perfect" society. In a bid to restore the timeline, Marty must travel back to 1876. In the game's climactic ending, three different DeLoreans arrive, each driven by a future version of Marty. They all insist that Doc and the present-day Marty assist them in preserving their respective futures. Rather than immediately intervening, Doc and Marty leave the future Martys to argue, deciding that the future can wait while they enjoy the present.

In a special moment for fans, Michael J. Fox lent his voice to the three alternate versions of Marty as well as William McFly. In celebration of the franchise's thirtieth anniversary, an updated version of the game was released on October 13, 2015, featuring the voice talents of Tom Wilson, finally giving fans the Biff Tannen experience they had hoped for.

Picking back up on the idea of a comic book series, Gale knew there were some more fun *Future* stories to tell. In 2015, IDW released the first issue of the comic series *Untold Tales and Alternate Timelines* on October 21, famously known as Future Day. The series was the brainchild of Bob Gale, who explained his motivation in a press release:

> We've subtitled this "Untold Tales and Alternate Timelines" because for years, fans have asked questions about things that happened before the events of the trilogy, in between the events of the trilogy, or in our alternate realities. In this series, we'll finally answer some of those questions, with our focus squarely on the characters everyone loves.

One of the most anticipated questions answered in the comic series was one that had long puzzled fans: How did a teenage boy like Marty McFly become best friends with a much older, eccentric scientist like Doc Brown? *Back to the Future* is known for meticulously explaining many aspects of the story—why the mall was named Twin Pines, how the flux capacitor was conceived, how Marty's parents met and fell in love—but the origin of Marty and Doc's friendship remained a mystery.

Fans finally got their answer in the issue titled "When Marty Met Emmett." The comic tells the story of how Marty, in October 1982, crossed paths with Douglas J. Needles, his high school rival and lead singer of The Tabascos. When a tube blew in Needles' guitar amp, he and his gang attempted to steal one from Marty. Failing in that attempt, they took Marty's guitar instead and demanded he find a replacement amp tube. Marty, desperate to get his guitar back, learned that the last available tube had been sold to ELB Enterprises. Tracking down Doc Brown (who owned ELB), Marty embarked on a series of misadventures that eventually led to the birth of their friendship. From then on, Marty, Doc, and Einstein were inseparable, their bond cemented in the space-time continuum.

This storyline was based on a long-standing rumor about the origins of Marty and Doc's friendship that Gale had previously hinted at. Responding to fan questions online, Gale once told *Mental Floss*:

> For years, Marty was told that Doc Brown was dangerous, a crackpot, a lunatic. So, being a red-blooded American teenage boy, age thirteen or fourteen, he decided to find out just why this guy was so dangerous. Marty snuck into Doc's lab and was fascinated by all the cool stuff that was there. When Doc found him, he was delighted that Marty thought he was cool and accepted him for what he was. Both of them were the black sheep in their respective environments. Doc gave Marty a part-time job to help with experiments, tend to the lab, and take care of the dog. And that's the origin of their relationship.

The *Back to the Future* animated series, the video game, and the subsequent comic books published by Harvey Comics and later by IDW gave fans even more opportunities to immerse themselves in the *Back to the Future* universe. These expansions allowed audiences to reconnect with the characters they loved—Doc, Marty, Biff—and experience new adventures that continued to grow the rich lore of Hill Valley. For hardcore fans, the animated series, the video game, and comics became essential parts of the *Back to the Future* experience, keeping the world of time travel alive and vibrant.

For those looking to explore even deeper into the *Back to the Future* universe, the IDW comic *Biff to the Future* is a must-read. This series delves into Biff Tannen's rise to power in the alternate 1985 timeline and explores more about the corrupt figure we see in *Back to the Future Part II*. Bob Gale continued to craft new layers of the *Back to the Future* mythology through these comics, giving fans more time with the characters they know and love.

These stories not only bring more depth to the *Back to the Future* universe but also allow fans to continue exploring Hill Valley and beyond. Whether through the adventures of Marty and Doc or the rise of Biff, the comic series keeps the spirit of the films alive and ensures the future of *Back to the Future* remains bright.

LETTERS FROM YOUR FRIENDS IN TIME: TONY RUSCOE

Founder of Back to the Future The Musical Fans

I've been a huge fan of *Back to the Future* since Christmas 1988 when it first aired on British TV (complete with terrible dubbing over the bad language) which fortunately meant I only had to wait a couple of years before watching *Part II* and *Part III* at my local multiplex cinema. Over the next few decades, my childhood collection of *Back to the Future* VHS tapes, DVDs, cassettes, CDs, books, models, collectibles, and prop replicas continued to grow along with my passion for the franchise.

As a child, I customized Lego minifigures to look like Doc and Marty, and reenacted scenes from the movie in a Lego version of Hill Valley. I made a flux capacitor out of a plastic box and cardboard and did my best to make my own hoverboard from memory out of plywood painted pink and Mattel logos cut from toy catalogs.

Soon after *Part II* was released to rent on VHS, I acquired a copy from a rental store. The tape was a little damaged toward the end when Marty burns the almanac but it quickly became my most-watched VHS tape and I soon realized how inaccurate my hoverboard was. (I made another one which years later made an appearance in a school production of *The Christmas Carol* when *The Ghost of Christmas*

Future entered with it hanging from some invisible thread which gave the appearance of it actually hovering!)

I was eventually able to replace my worn-out rental copy of *Part II* with the limited edition widescreen VHS box set of the trilogy which included *The Secrets of the Back to the Future Trilogy.* Twenty minutes of bonus material was great, but I desperately wanted to know more about the making of the trilogy, so I was ecstatic to find a copy of *Back to the Future: The Official Book of the Complete Movie Trilogy* by Michael Klastorin at my school book sale in 1990. I read it so much that all of the pages came loose and I had to punch holes in them and rebind it.

Over the next few years, my collection of memorabilia continued to grow. I bought the *Original Motion Picture Soundtrack* for both *Part II* and *Part III* on audio cassette. My best friend visited Universal Studios and sent me a postcard featuring Back to the Future: The Ride, which I unfortunately never got to experience. I built the Halcyon plastic 1:24 model of the DeLorean time machine from *Part III* and added Corgi and Sunstar die-cast models to my birthday and Christmas wish lists. As the trilogy was released and re-released in new formats with new bonus material each year, my collection gained multiple DVD box sets which I watched on repeat (who else remembers the BTTF DVD Framing Fiasco?) and I finally got to own the complete score for *Back to the Future* when the *Intrada Special Collection* two-CD limited edition was released.

In 2010, I was able to watch the original *Back to the Future* movie on the big screen for the first time when it was re-released in UK cinemas to coincide with the movie's twenty-fifth anniversary and the Blu-ray release. Fans in the queue could be heard arguing about which film in the trilogy was the best while others quoted their favorite lines. The film started with a spontaneous round of applause and cheering followed by complete silence as everyone watched Marty enter Doc's lab in the opening scene. (Five years later, I watched all three movies back-to-back when they were re-released at cinemas on October 21st, 2015, in celebration of Future Day.)

It feels like the twenty-fifth anniversary was the start of a second wave for *Back to the Future*'s popularity as I acquired more and more merchandise, including an officially licensed full-scale prop replica Mattel Hoverboard complete with swooshing sound effects. But my collection really exploded when I discovered *The RPF* forums in 2012 and found its talented members were making and selling screen accurate prop replicas of everything from *Grays Sports Almanac*, the *Oh LàLà* magazine, the *Tales from Space* comic book and *Hill Valley Telegraph* newspapers to the foil Pizza Hut bags, dehydrated pizzas, and Pepsi Perfect bottles.

Being able to hold some of these prop replicas in my hands really felt like a piece of Hill Valley had come to life, but that was taken to the next level when I attended Secret Cinema Presents *Back to the Future* in 2014. This was an immersive event in London, where around eighty actors and detailed set pieces welcomed guests to the 1955 Hill Valley Town Fair before an outdoor screening of the movie was projected onto the Hill Valley Courthouse while actors and stunt performers performed key scenes live and in sync with the movie. Bob Gale was in attendance and congratulated the production team on an "absolutely fantastic" experience!

In 2015, I had the pleasure of attending the world premiere of *Back to the Future* Live in Concert in Switzerland before it embarked on a tour of major concert venues around the world in celebration of the thirtieth anniversary. This is a special screening of *Back to the Future* accompanied by a live orchestra, performing an adaptation of the score featuring an additional fifteen minutes composed exclusively by Alan Silvestri for parts of the movie which weren't originally accompanied by any music. I met Alan for the first time in the lobby before the performance and thanked him for creating such a wonderful score.

Rumors about a stage adaptation had been circulating since around 2012. When news finally broke that the musical would premiere in Manchester in February 2020, I grabbed tickets for the opening weekend and planned a trip with my family. What I watched exceeded all of my expectations. I don't think I stopped grinning from the first moment I saw Doc's lab until the mind-blowing finale. The casting was perfect, the songs and lyrics were instantly memorable, and the special effects were incredible. I really appreciated the attention to detail that went into the sets, props, and costumes, and was thrilled to hear so much of the iconic dialogue and original score from the movie being reused. It simultaneously felt very familiar and yet it was brand new!

I created the Back to the Future The Musical Fans group on Facebook the following day so that I could share and discuss the whole experience with others. Despite the Manchester run being canceled just three weeks later due to COVID, the group continued to gain new members and I created our Twitter and Instagram accounts in October 2020 in preparation for the show reopening in London's West End in 2021.

Together with Angela Smith, we've continued to build the community and share the latest news and updates about *Back to the Future: The Musical*. We've interviewed Bob Gale, Alan Silvestri and Glen Ballard, as well as multiple cast members from the West End production, which we publish to our YouTube channel and podcast. And when the Broadway production was announced in 2022, we created a separate Back to the Future Broadway Fans group and accompanying social media accounts to focus on the Broadway and North American Tour productions. I also created the *Back to the Future: The Musical Wiki*, a community-maintained website dedicated to sharing knowledge and information about all of the *Back to the Future: The Musical* productions around the world.

Being so passionate about *Back to the Future: The Musical* has allowed us to develop a good relationship with the production team, who have kindly invited us to attend press nights and gala performances. In July 2023, we were honored to attend the Michael J. Fox Foundation Gala Performance in New York alongside Bob Gale, Alan Silvestri, Glen Ballard, Robert Zemeckis, Steven Spielberg, Huey Lewis, Michael J. Fox, Christopher Lloyd, Lea Thompson, Marc McClure, James Tolkan, Don Fullilove, and Harry Waters Jr!

It's safe to say that *Back to the Future* has had a huge presence in my life. Over the years many friends and family members have asked why I love *Back to the Future* so much and I never truly know how to answer. It just feels like *Back to the Future* has been a part of my life for as long as I can remember and I can't imagine what my life would have been like without it. I'm pretty sure that nine-year-old me never imagined that thirty-five years into the future he would still be a huge fan of *Back to the Future*, still adding to his collection, constantly making new friends from the fandom, and traveling the world to watch it being performed on stage!

Your Friend in Time,

Tony Ruscoe

CHAPTER 6

THE POWER OF LOVE AND MUSIC

So, there we were, getting ready to head to the entertainment capital of the world—New York City. We landed the night before we were scheduled to see *Back to the Future: The Musical*. I got into a taxi at LaGuardia, crossing the New Jersey Turnpike, and as we pulled up to our weekend hotel, The Public Hotel, I was excited for the next day, and something that I had looked forward to for so, so long.

What made it even better was that, although my wife isn't as big of a *Back to the Future* fan as I am, she was equally excited. That's the great thing about marriage—you get excited for each other's passions. Her support for me was infectious, and I was even more hyped because of it. You end up loving what your partner loves—if that makes sense. I hope it does.

The night before the play, as I laid my head down, I had that same feeling I used to get on Christmas Eve as a kid—the kind of sleep where you keep turning over, checking the clock, looking for daylight so you can rush to wake everyone up and tear into the presents. That night wasn't a regular sleep; it was an excited, restless sleep filled with anticipation for what was to come.

I woke up the next morning, counting down the hours like I knew when lightning would strike the clock tower. I could feel it coming, and I just wanted the moment to arrive.

We spent the day exploring, but then the time came. We got into the Uber and headed to Broadway. As we pulled up on that crisp October evening—thirty-eight years after the events of *Back to the Future Part I*—I was giddy. Despite the cold, my excitement kept me warm. My wife and I took pictures in front of the marquee that proudly displayed *Back to the Future: The Musical*, and as we entered the theater, I was speed-walking like one of those Olympic walkers! (By the way, did you know speed-walking is an Olympic sport? To quote Rodney Dangerfield when he ran into Eddie Murphy in Las Vegas at Eddie's peak after telling Eddie when he was younger to clean up his act..."Who knew?")

Nevertheless, I couldn't wait to see the stage. Working in media and professional wrestling, I've been to my fair share of major events—WrestleMania, Royal Rumble, Survivor Series—and I've always been eager to see the production design at these events. And now, here I was, speed-walking into a Broadway theater, eager to see what awaited me.

I might not be a high-society type—just a Southern boy from Texas—but I do love live stage productions. My wife and I try to hit the theater as often as we can, whether it's at the Hobby Center or the Alley Theater in Houston or flying to Broadway. Just before this trip, we saw Pamela Anderson in *Chicago* and let me tell you—she nailed it! But walking into that theater for *Back to the Future: The Musical*, I felt my excitement reach levels I didn't think possible.

I took in every detail: the stage, the lighting, the preshow atmosphere. And then—bam—it began. The lights went down, the spotlights hit the stage, and it was all happening. Something I had dreamed of, talked about, and thought about was finally real.

The production value blew me away. I've seen several Broadway shows, but this one had an insane amount of money invested in it. Every element was executed with precision—music, set design, performances—it was beyond brilliant. Like, brilliant times a googolplex.

From Marty's first appearance to Doc to the DeLorean itself, there wasn't a single moment I wasn't completely in love with. When intermission hit, my wife looked at me with wide eyes, waiting for my reaction. But before I could share my thoughts, I overheard a conversation in the row ahead of us. A father, probably in his mid-forties, asked his son—no older than seven or eight—what he thought. The boy was practically glowing with excitement as he exclaimed, "Dad, this is so awesome."

I turned to my wife and smiled because that moment right there—that pure, unfiltered joy—is why this story, this *Back to the Future* journey, has stood the test of time. It's generational. Everyone, from a young kid to an adult, finds themselves swept up in the adventure. Maybe as a kid, you don't ponder the deeper questions about time travel or your parents' lives, but you think the DeLorean is awesome. You feel Marty's anxiety about getting back to 1985, and you root for him every step of the way.

When the second half started, I was completely absorbed again. The songs didn't feel like fillers; they moved the story forward, adding depth to Marty, George, Doc, and even Jennifer. I was watching with a critical eye, trying to find any flaw I could. I mean, nothing's perfect, right? But *Back to the Future: The Musical* came pretty damn close.

Of course, any adaptation from screen to stage requires some changes, and I expected that. But those changes—let me tell you—they were creative and refreshing, even for a long-time fan like me. It's like the team behind this show didn't just throw it together for a cash grab (cough, cough, *Harry Potter and the Cursed Child*). Bob Gale, Bob Zemeckis, Alan Silvestri—all the original creatives—they thought this through, and it showed.

The updates to the story were great, and, in some cases, even enhanced it. Whether you were a first-time viewer like that kid in the audience or a hardcore fan like me, it was an incredible experience.

As we left the theater that night, I had to decompress. I was buzzing from what I had just seen. And as always, when I become obsessed with something, I have to start researching—learning everything about the origins of this musical.

Before I saw the musical, I had already purchased a phenomenal book that would help me get more information about what I had just seen. And while it may not be commonplace for one book to recommend another, as you've already seen, I do that throughout this work. So, allow me to illuminate another one for you—*Creating Back to the Future: The Musical* by Michael Klastorin.

This book had been sitting on my desk in Houston while I was in New York, preparing to see *Back to the Future: The Musical* for the first time. I purposefully did not open it before seeing the musical to avoid any spoilers. Nevertheless, this is the ultimate history of *Back to the Future: The Musical*, and what I will touch on in this chapter doesn't do justice to the wealth of information contained in this incredible book. So, again, after reading my thoughts and learning about the origin of the musical, I highly recommend you purchase *Creating Back to the Future: The Musical.*

While reading this book, I discovered several fascinating things. First, in the prologue, Michael delves into the origins of *Back to the Future: The Musical.* Naturally, you might assume that they were looking for some way to continue the story—not as a remake, reboot, or sequel to the film trilogy, but as a continuation of the *Back to the Future* mythos, similar to what they've done with the comic books or the *Back to the Future* animated series. I assumed this idea had been cooking in one, if not both, of the Bobs' (Robert Zemeckis and Bob Gale) minds for years. However, that's not what happened at all.

The origins of *Back to the Future: The Musical* started at the James Theatre in New York City in 2005. Robert Zemeckis, along with his incredibly talented wife, Leslie Zemeckis—a filmmaker and author (her most recent documentary, *Grande Horizontals,* is something I highly recommend)—were attending a performance of *The Producers,* starring Nathan Lane and Matthew Broderick. The cheers could be heard from the audience inside the theater on West 44th Street. While experiencing the raucous ovation from the crowd, Leslie Zemeckis turned to her husband and said, "You should make *Back to the Future* into a musical."

Leslie didn't think she was saying anything revolutionary, but her words stuck with Robert. As we've discussed, both Zemeckis and Gale had always maintained that they never wanted to make a *Back to the Future Part IV.* When the words "The End" appeared on screen at the conclusion of *Back to the Future Part III,* they both felt the trilogy had reached a satisfying conclusion.

Yet, the idea of adapting *Back to the Future* into a stage play—and not just any stage play, but a musical—intrigued Robert Zemeckis enough that he began to seriously consider it. And of course, he wanted to share this concept with his good friend and collaborator Bob Gale.

When Bob Gale first heard the idea he didn't dismiss it outright. In fact, he remarked that while it wasn't something that had ever occurred to him, he surprisingly didn't hate it. Gale admitted this was his usual reaction to most *Back to the Future* pitches, many of which often felt like obvious money grabs. But this wasn't just any *Back to the Future* pitch. This came from Leslie Zemeckis, an avid fan of theater and musicals.

Because of Leslie's unique perspective, Bob Gale decided to seriously consider the idea. After seeing *The Producers* film and talking over the concept with his wife, Tina, Gale looked more into taking this baby up to eighty-eight miles per hour. Maybe this wasn't just a passing thought. Maybe there was something here. Gale started to think—if they could explore the possibilities of adapting *Back to the Future* into a musical, it might be more than just a novelty act. It could be a new way to introduce the story to a different generation, while also giving long-time fans something fresh.

If there's one thing that's obvious about *Back to the Future* fans, it's that we love the trilogy so much that we're always hungry for more. Our appetite for the films and their world is insatiable. Both Bobs knew this. They also knew that they alone held the keys to the *Back to the Future* kingdom and, quite literally, the future of this beloved IP. With this in mind, the two Bobs began to tinker with the idea of turning their iconic film into a full-fledged musical.

The Bobs knew, however, that this wouldn't be a simple task. You couldn't just slap the *Back to the Future* name on a musical and expect it to be good. It would take work. It would take effort. It would take years of planning. And more importantly, they knew they couldn't do it alone. If they brought *Back to the Future* to the stage, they needed someone who had helped shape the sound of the future. They needed Alan Silvestri.

Of course, Alan Silvestri had done a lot since *Back to the Future*. He had provided the score for the biggest box-office franchise of all time—the *Avengers* films in the Marvel Cinematic Universe. He had won Grammys and Emmys and been nominated for multiple Oscars. If there was going to be a *Back to the Future* musical, Alan Silvestri was the one person they had to involve.

The collaboration between Silvestri, Gale, and Zemeckis began, and with the original creative team on board, the wheels were in motion. However, it still wasn't enough. The Bobs knew they needed someone from the world of theater who could take their beloved film and reimagine it for the stage. Enter Glen Ballard, the six-time Grammy Award–winning lyricist and producer who had worked with the likes of Alanis Morissette and Quincy Jones.

Glen Ballard is, without a doubt, a music legend. A six-time Grammy winner, Ballard's career is a testament to his immense talent and versatility. In 2023, he was inducted into the Songwriters Hall of Fame and selected to receive a star on the Hollywood Walk of Fame. Beyond the artists already mentioned, Ballard has written and produced songs for iconic figures like Aretha Franklin, Shakira, Katy Perry, Ringo Starr, George Strait, and Van Halen—just to name a few.

One of Ballard's most famous contributions to music was co-writing and arranging "Man in the Mirror" for Michael Jackson. This success set the stage for another pivotal moment in his career. In 2004, Robert

Zemeckis was working on *The Polar Express*, with Alan Silvestri composing the score. Silvestri suggested that Zemeckis collaborate with Glen Ballard, believing that their respective successes—Silvestri in scoring and Ballard in songwriting and production—would be a perfect match. Their collaboration resulted in the Academy Award–nominated and Grammy Award–winning song "Believe," performed by Josh Groban. Glen understood how to make a story sing—literally. His contributions to the lyrics and musical arrangement, alongside Silvestri's compositions, ensured that *Back to the Future: The Musical* wasn't just a rehash of the movie but a full-blown musical experience with original songs that could stand on their own.

When Bob Gale, Robert Zemeckis, and Alan Silvestri began crafting *Back to the Future: The Musical*, Glen Ballard naturally became part of that core creative team. On February 5, 2007, the group met at Robert Zemeckis's office in Carpinteria, California, to officially kick off the project. From the beginning, they all agreed that a straight adaptation of the film wouldn't work. It had to be different to engage audiences, and creativity would be key.

There were many ideas pitched early on about how to best adapt the story for the stage. This approach encouraged the team to explore fresh angles for *Back to the Future*. Silvestri knew this collaboration would be fruitful because both Bob Gale and Robert Zemeckis were always open to hearing new story ideas. Silvestri and Ballard dove into their work, watching *Back to the Future* dozens of times to determine the best spots for musical numbers and what the songs should convey. Before long, music and lyrics were in development, along with a reimagined script.

As this core group worked tirelessly to bring *Back to the Future* to the stage, all while balancing other projects, numerous challenges began to surface. Creative differences with partners and collaborators, including director Jamie Lloyd, delayed the musical adaptation beyond its projected start date. An article from *Broadway World* on August 28, 2014, reported that Jamie Lloyd had parted ways with the *Back to the Future* musical just before workshops were set to begin in Los Angeles and London. The split was due to disagreements between Lloyd and Bob Gale regarding the direction of the production.

Lloyd was quoted in *The Daily Mail* as saying, "It's just a case of wanting to stand by my vision...you absolutely have to believe in it, or there's not much point." Following Lloyd's departure, Gale took over rewriting the musical, with plans to send a new draft to directors by the following year, aiming for a 2016 debut in London's West End. Initially, the team had hoped to launch *Back to the Future: The Musical* in 2015, aligning with the film's thirtieth anniversary—a fittingly futuristic milestone. However, the delays meant that this vision would need to wait.

Eventually, John Rando was chosen as the director for *Back to the Future: The Musical.* A Tony Award winner for his 2002 production of *Urinetown*, Rando had several other directorial credits on Broadway, particularly in shows adapted from films or productions that had gone back and forth between the stage and screen. His résumé included works like *A Christmas Story, The Wedding Singer, A Thousand Clowns*, and *On the Town.*

After Rando met with Gale and Ballard, they felt confident they had found their director. Both Zemeckis and Silvestri were fully on board with Gale and Ballard's recommendation, and on February 20, 2018, John Rando officially became the director of *Back to the Future: The Musical.* With Rando in place, the workshops began, as did the search for the perfect cast.

The two most significant casting choices were, of course, for Doc Brown and Marty McFly. Roger Bart became the first actor, other than Christopher Lloyd, to take on the iconic live-action role of Doc Emmett L. Brown on the stage or screen. Bart, a seasoned actor with dozens of film credits, including 2013's *Last Vegas* (which also featured *Back to the Future* alum Mary Steenburgen), was no stranger to the stage either. He provided the singing voice for *Hercules* in Disney's 1997 film and starred in *The Producers*, both in the film and on stage, earning a Tony Award nomination for his performance as Carmen Ghia. Bart also won a Tony in 1999 for *You're a Good Man, Charlie Brown*, and little did he know that taking on the role of Doc Brown would earn him his third Tony nomination for Best Featured Actor in a Musical for *Back to the Future: The Musical*.

The role of Marty McFly was next on the list. In 2014, the audition process began, and one of the early standouts was a graduate from the London Arts Educational Schools—a young actor named Olly Dobson. Auditioning for Marty was Dobson's first audition since graduating, and he wasn't sure what to expect from the process. However, he showed so much promise that he was called back six additional times for readings. Despite his talent, Dobson ultimately lost the role to another actor from New York.

But when casting reopened in 2018, Dobson was determined to portray Marty McFly—it felt like it might have been his destiny. When casting the perfect Marty McFly, the director, John Rando, had specific qualifications in mind. The actor needed to have a great singing voice, the right look, and the right style, period. Rando saw all of these qualities in Olly Dobson. He later remarked that Dobson's portrayal respected Michael J. Fox's iconic performance, while still allowing Dobson to make the role his own.

Dobson worked closely with Rando to develop the character, participating in the crucial workshop phase—leading to a bare-bones presentation of the musical. This step is essential in the production process, as it often leads to a formal casting offer if the performance resonates with the creative team. When Olly Dobson was officially offered the role of Marty McFly, he was, in his own words, "over the moon." After years of perseverance, Dobson finally secured the iconic role that would define his stage career.

On May 17, 2019, a press release was sent to media outlets around the world, announcing in bold letters: "*Back to the Future: The Musical* to open at Manchester Opera House on Thursday, February 20, 2020, for a twelve-week season." The time circuits were on, and the production was speeding up to eighty-eight miles per hour, racing toward the highly anticipated opening of *Back to the Future: The Musical.*

On February 20, 2020, previews for *Back to the Future: The Musical* began. After years of delays, fans eagerly filtered into the Manchester Opera House to see their favorite film brought to life on stage. The production was directed by John Rando, with choreography by Chris Bailey, set and costume design by Tim Hatley, video designs by Finn Ross, lighting by Tim Lutkin and Hugh Vanstone, and sound design by Gareth Owen.

In an episode of *Back to the Future: The Podcast*, I had the chance to sit down with Tony Ruscoe and Angela Smith, who recounted their experience seeing *Back to the Future: The Musical* during this exciting time. Both Angela and Tony were there on press night on March 11, 2020, the official opening in Manchester.

ANGELA: It was just electric the whole day. Like we said, there'd been a pre-event at Piccadilly Gardens, and there were loads of fans there, all buzzing with excitement. Having Bob [Gale] and Alan [Silvestri] there really built up the anticipation, and I remember the cast—it was just building from that moment on. My friend and I went to a bar near the theater, and it was packed with fans, all talking about the show. Everyone had *Back to the Future* T-shirts on, and you could easily spot other fans and say, "Oh, you're going to the show too!" There was such a buzz.

By the time we got to the theater, it was truly electric. There were railings set up for everyone to watch the creatives and celebrities arrive. We were all pressed up against the barrier, watching them get photographed. And when we finally got into the foyer, it was just as exciting. The queue for the merch stands was enormous, with everyone trying to get as much as they possibly could. The atmosphere was absolutely incredible—everyone was there for the same purpose, and the fans made sure to blow the roof off the theater. The energy was palpable, and it still gives me goosebumps when I think about it. It was the most amazing night.

TONY: I had no idea what to expect. And even then, especially then, because there's no production photography, there were no trailers—there were a couple of music videos out where they were just in a studio singing, so you got to hear a couple of the tracks, but apart from that, you really did not know what to expect. I think they had some rehearsal footage where they were in a studio environment, no set pieces, maybe a frame of a DeLorean they were wheeling around.

> But that moment, the first scene in Doc's garage, from that moment right through to the finale, my face was just aching from grinning. There was no point when I stopped smiling, just being completely immersed in what was happening. And to be honest, with each different iteration of it, the same feeling was there. So, when they opened in London, when they did the cast change in London, they made slight tweaks, and when they opened on Broadway, they made some tweaks. But with every single one, it's like seeing it again for the first time with a brand-new cast and a new refreshing take on it. So, you still get that first-watch feeling again and again whenever you go and see it.

The musical was off to a great start, but just days after press night, the fire trails were extinguished. On Saturday, March 14, 2020, the end of *Back to the Future: The Musical*'s opening week concluded with a Saturday evening performance. Colin Ingram, the lead producer of the musical, was closely monitoring the news at the time. He recalled the Prime Minister addressing the nation on Sunday, March 15, 2020, around five p.m. Just an hour later, the Society of London Theatre, the industry's governing body, declared that all theaters should shut down, following the government's advice.

On Monday, March 16, Ingram sent an email to every member of the *Back to the Future* production. He expressed regret that the musical's run would be suspended due to the ongoing pandemic. COVID-19 had shocked the world—including the Future world. That same day, *Back to the Future: The Musical* posted an announcement that read:

> We regret to announce that from this evening, the Manchester Opera House has closed in light of official government advice. Back to the Future: The Musical performances are therefore suspended until further notice. Your box office/retailer from

> whom you bought your tickets will be in contact with regards to refunds and exchanges. Please bear with us during these unprecedented times.

And unprecedented times they were. The Saturday evening performance became the last for the year—and the last in Manchester for the time being.

Fast forward over a year later to July 19, 2021, when the first full rehearsal of *Back to the Future: The Musical*'s London engagement took place at the National Youth Theatre. With the pandemic easing, the show was preparing for its long-awaited return. The production of *Back to the Future: The Musical* officially opened in the West End on September 13, 2021, at the Adelphi Theatre in London, featuring the same principal cast and crew that had begun the journey in Manchester. After a successful run in the UK, the musical finally made its way stateside, with preview performances beginning June 30, 2023 and an official Broadway debut on August 3, 2023, at the Winter Garden Theatre, where I finally got to experience *Back to the Future: The Musical* firsthand.

As with any adaptation, certain elements from a movie don't always translate smoothly to the stage, especially when it comes to a story like *Back to the Future*, which many—including myself—consider perfect. For instance, in *Back to the Future: The Musical*, Doc Brown doesn't have his faithful dogs, Einstein or Copernicus. This is likely due to the difficulty of controlling live animals night after night or the potential awkwardness of using animatronics for the dogs on stage.

Another significant change involves a new invention from Doc—a device that recognizes Marty and leaves him messages. This adds a fresh layer to their relationship, while the story also introduces Jennifer

Parker's Uncle Huey, who is set to help Marty and his band—a fun nod to Huey Lewis. The absence of the Libyan terrorists from the movie is another noteworthy adaptation. Instead, Doc dies from radiation poisoning, which makes sense in today's context. This change addresses modern cultural sensitivities and avoids the challenge of staging a chase scene like the one at Twin Pines Mall.

In this version, Doc's faulty radiation suit leads to his sudden poisoning, which sets off Marty's race to save him by getting to the hospital in the DeLorean—and, of course, hitting eighty-eight miles per hour. The time machine is also voice-activated, and only Doc can operate it, creating an additional complication later when Marty needs to start the car and can't.

Other differences include the absence of Old Man Peabody and the omission of the famous "Darth Vader from the Planet Vulcan" scene. Interestingly, in this version, George falls on Marty, instead of Marty pushing George out of the way when Lorraine's dad's car is about to strike him. And when Marty tells Doc in 1955 that Ronald Reagan is president in 1985, instead of asking if Jerry Lewis is vice president, Doc asks if the vice president is Daffy Duck (sometimes Doc substitutes Daffy for Pepé Le Pew, Porky Pig, or Sylvester the Cat).

Additionally, there's no iconic skateboarding chase scene, likely for the same reasons there's no large chase at the mall. Marvin Berry doesn't call his cousin Chuck (this part of the musical was cut in the Manchester previews), and instead of playing a passive role, Goldie Wilson actively helps Doc Brown set up the wires for the climactic science experiment to send Marty back to the future.

The final scene of the musical also diverges from the film's ending. In *Back to the Future: The Musical*, instead of Marty arriving back in

1985 to find George McFly in a newly furnished home, unveiling his brand-new book *A Match Made in Space*, the ending features a town hall celebration for "George McFly Day" to launch his latest book titled *Back to the Future 4*. This playful twist on the original ending changes the tone of the conclusion, adding a new layer of humor for fans of the franchise.

I spoke with Eric Tate, proprietor of CollectBTTF.com, and Tony Ruscoe from Back to the Future The Musical Fans to get their thoughts on this new ending and the self-referential *Back to the Future* joke during a podcast nerding out on all things the BTTF musical.

> **ERIC:** I loved it. It's another one of those things—I wanted to be surprised by this. I didn't want them to just put the same movie up on the stage and be like, 'Then what's coming?' So this was a welcome change. I loved the whole setup, and I think they really did a great job, just like in the movie, of showing the transformation of George McFly—from a non-confident teenager to a confident, well-kept man, father, and husband. It really shows what a great person he becomes.
>
> And I also think, and maybe I'm thinking too much into this, but I know there was a lot of controversy after *Back to the Future Part I* regarding Crispin Glover and how George McFly was portrayed—how it seemed like money made him happy, and all that stuff. But in the musical, I feel like the ending focuses less on the financial side of things. Sure, they mention the check and all, but the emphasis is more on George just being a well-rounded, genuinely happy person. As far as the stage adaptation goes, I felt it was a very satisfying conclusion.

TONY: I think Eric's got a good point there. They touch on the money, but it's more like the McFly family is doing something good with their wealth, like giving it to the Clock Tower Preservation Society. They're part of the community. It's not just about them being rich and buying a four-by-four for their son—there's no mention of that in the musical. So I think they balanced it out well.

Also, from a practical standpoint, it wouldn't have worked to go from the town square to Twin Pines Mall and then back to Lyon Estates on stage. You couldn't do that many set changes. But the novel joke they included—it's hilarious. It's a proper in-joke for anyone who knows about *Back to the Future* and all the reboots. Early on, they called it *Back to the Future 2* because, well, you're watching *Back to the Future*, so it's like the sequel's already been written. I think I read somewhere that it was Alan Silvestri who suggested they should make it *Back to the Future 4*, and everyone agreed that was a perfect joke. It works well—just great.

Back to the Future: The Musical is a much-welcomed addition to the *Back to the Future* universe, one that fans will enjoy for generations, as the great song says, "for all time." If you want to dive deeper into the making of the musical, let me again recommend *Creating Back to the Future: The Musical* by Michael Klastorin, an incredibly researched and beautifully crafted book about this remarkable production.

We've now seen the *Back to the Future* story continue in many forms: through the Back to the Future: The Ride at Universal Studios, the animated series, the comic books, and now the musical. But now it's time to look back—back to what happened on Future Day in 2015, at scenes that were left on the cutting room floor and could have changed *Back to the Future* forever. We'll revisit some of our favorite inventions from Doc Brown, reconnect with some of our favorite friends in time, and ponder what the future truly has in store.

LETTERS FROM YOUR FRIENDS IN TIME: ERIC TATE

Creator of CollectBTTF.com

My journey within the incomparable world of *Back to the Future* started when I was very young. Being almost the same age as the franchise itself, I didn't have the experience of seeing the films during their premieres and instead fell in love with them through the VHS box set in my parents' movie collection. I don't specifically remember the first time I watched the movies, but I do remember quickly being captivated by every aspect of them.

As I grew, so did my love for *Back to the Future*. I would watch the trilogy often and discover additional nuances with each viewing that made me appreciate it even more for the masterpiece that it is. The films were—and continue to be—perfect for any scenario I find myself in. Whether I was happy and looking for a feel-good time or needing a break from reality, *Back to the Future* was always there to supplement my mood or help me get through it.

The internet brought my love for *Back to the Future* to levels I could never have predicted. I still distinctly remember logging into AOL as a kid and searching for new ways to connect with information about *Back to the Future* and others who shared my fascination. Countless hours were spent absorbing new information like a sponge. But the largest component that turned my love into an obsession was when I discovered the fan site BTTF.com, especially its forums. The site was founded by the wonderful Stephen Clark and served as the most comprehensive source for *Back to the Future* information available, eventually evolving into the official BacktotheFuture.com website. Suddenly, I wasn't alone! The site's forums became my most visited site for years to come. I would get lost in conversations and learn something new with each refresh.

In 2002, I was excited by the news that the *Back to the Future* trilogy was going to be released on DVD for the first time. This was especially wonderful as my VHS copies had seen better days. I promptly picked up a copy on release day and began wondering what other types of *Back to the Future* merchandise might be out there. Little did I know that scoping things out and picking up a random collectible here and there would turn into a very large hobby.

While planning a 2006 vacation to California, news broke about the impending closure of Back to the Future: The Ride at Universal Studios Florida. I had never been to Florida, nor had I had the opportunity to ride the greatest theme park attraction of all time, so I immediately knew that my vacation plans were changing. After riding the thrilling adventure over and over again, I went into the *Back to the Future* gift shop and said to the employee, *"You may want to clear some counter space because I'm leaving here with at least one of every Back to the Future item you have."* I stayed true to my word—so true to it that I didn't even have enough space in my luggage for all the items! After returning home, I promptly got a new bookcase for my bedroom and consolidated all of my *Back to the Future* memorabilia on it. From then on, it became a goal to collect as much *Back to the Future* memorabilia as I could.

As I continued to grow older, *Back to the Future* began shaping portions of my life and bleeding into the relationships I have with others. Marvin Berry and the Starlighters' rendition of "Earth Angel" was my wife's and my wedding song; I've made great friends throughout the *Back to the Future* community, and I've even gotten to make connections with members of the cast and crew involved in the franchise. It's all been a true blessing—one I don't take for granted.

But nothing has been more rewarding than getting to share my passion with my children. Whether it's watching the movies, binging the animated series, simulating The Ride, playing with the toys, listening to the soundtracks, or taking a trip to Broadway to watch *Back to the Future: The Musical*, my kids have become card-carrying members of the next generation of *Back to the Future* fans. My daughter has even started her own hoverboard collection! My wife and I are raising our children to be kind, confident, and passionate individuals who know that they can accomplish anything if they just put their minds to it.

I knew for a while that I wanted to find a way to give back to the community that has given me so much. After being inspired by the wonderful *Back to the Future Almanac* by Rob Klein and Jennifer Smith, I decided to begin working on a website that would give fans an extensive look into the history of *Back to the Future* collectibles as well as act as a hub for fellow fans to show off their collections. CollectBTTF.com launched in 2023 and has so far cataloged over 1,500 pieces of *Back to the Future* history while also helping raise money for deserving charities. It's been an incredible full-circle feeling to be behind a new resource for fans. If it helps even one person in the way the resources I discovered as a kid helped me, it will have all been worth it.

Back to the Future has been my gateway to experiences I never could have imagined. It's a part of my life that I'm proud of and enjoy sharing with others. I'm grateful for all the joy it has brought me. It's the type of journey truly meant for the dreamers, like me.

Your Friend in Time,
Eric Tate

PART III

BACK IN TIME

CHAPTER 7

FUTURE DAY

When I first fell in love with these films as a child, the 1980s didn't resonate with me. Don't get me wrong—big hair, shoulder pads, and synth-pop music were cool and all. But as a child of the 1990s, it felt as though the 1980s were more my older siblings' time than mine. So, if 1985 felt old, imagine what I thought of 1955, another time period I could only experience through the films. Born in 1992, the 1950s were even more distant to me. But in *Back to the Future Part II*, I became fixated, like many others, on the year 2015 for several reasons. The biggest reason was how inspiring the Bobs made this time feel. It was hopeful, it was colorful, and it felt possible. What I mean by "possible" is that it felt conceivable to my adolescent mind. Heck, it was only a few years away, and I knew I would see a time period from the films for the first and only time.

With each passing year, I became more aware of the approach of 2015. I would track different items or inventions that resembled future tech from the *Back to the Future* version of 2015. Whether it was the introduction of "picture in picture" like Marty Jr. had on display in the future McFly Manor or Google Glass, which was awfully close to what Marty Sr.'s kids wore at the dinner table. I also noted Apple's introduction of Apple Pay in 2014, which lets users pay for items (such as a taxi to track down a couple of time travelers) with just a thumbprint, and the use of holograms for entertainment, such as the deceased rapper Tupac Shakur's holographic performance alongside Snoop Dogg at Coachella in 2012. Of course, some big predictions made in *Back to the Future Part II* have yet to occur, like flying cars and hoverboards sold by Mattel. But the inventions we did get were great examples of both Bobs being literal futurists. All fans of the franchise eagerly awaited the day that Marty and Doc would appear in 2015.

I began *Back to the Future: The Podcast* in 2015 largely to help ring in the day: October 21, 2015. Before I knew it, May turned into June, July, and then October 20. I went to sleep that evening the same way a young kid falls asleep on Christmas Eve—with one eye open and my imagination filled with wonder about what the next day would bring. When I woke up the next morning, I grabbed my phone and began scrolling through Twitter to see any news stories about Future Day and the accompanying festivities. I saw some of the usual memes and GIFs of Marty and Doc with the hashtag #FutureDay, along with tweets from famous actors and musicians celebrating the film. Upon searching that hashtag, I saw a man post a photo of himself reading a *USA Today* newspaper with the headline "Youth Jailed." Upon further inspection, it was the same newspaper that Doc held in his hand when explaining to Marty why they had to go to 2015 in the first place.

I did some further investigating to see where I could get a copy of *USA Today*. I noticed that the guy's Instagram post said he was at the Crowne Plaza in the Greenway area of Houston. For those unfamiliar with Houston, let alone the Lone Star State of Texas, if something isn't down the street from you—meaning on your block—you will have to get in a car and travel a bare minimum of thirty minutes to an hour to get where you are going. I instantly got into my silver Ford F-150, the Texas equivalent of the DeLorean, and tried to make my way to the Crowne Plaza to secure my copy. I navigated the always-congested Houston traffic and pulled up to the front of the hotel. I saw a valet driver ready to take my keys, but I avoided eye contact as I didn't have time to go through that process. I glanced down at my watch, feeling like Doc waiting for Marty to arrive at the clock tower from the Enchantment Under the Sea dance. I had to get to a meeting by 10:00. The time was 9:42. *Damn!*

After telling the valet to make like a tree and get out of here and driving around the lot, I realized there was no additional parking, so I had to decide fast. I saw a fire lane that clearly read "no parking at any time," but this wasn't any time. This was *the* time and the only chance I would have to accomplish this mission. I pulled into the fire lane, threw the truck in park, and turned the hazard lights on. I got out of the truck and glanced at my watch again: 9:48. *Damn! Damn!*

I began to walk to the entrance of the hotel and could see the valet trying to get my attention. I completely ignored him, jumped through the automatic doors, and asked the first hotel employee I saw where to buy a newspaper. The employee pointed toward the gift shop to my right, and I accelerated my pace with at least half the gigawatts needed to send a normal time machine to its preferred destination. I saw the gift shop a few steps away, but not far behind me was the valet driver, who was becoming my real-life Biff Tannen. I finally got to the gift shop and looked around quickly to locate the *USA Today*. I knew I was running out of time to get to my meeting, and I only had seconds before the valet driver would catch up to me. The gift shop looked more like Hill Valley High School in the alternate 1985 because there was nothing but empty racks where the newspapers should have been. It was barren, depressing, and empty. They were sold out.

I pivoted around in defeat, and before I could make a move, the valet driver was nearly nose-to-nose with me. By this time, the slightly overweight man with dark circles under his eyes and a golden name tag that read "Douglas" (last name not confirmed but assumed to be Needles) raised his voice to overdrive and said, "Excuse me, sir, you are not allowed to park out there. You need to move your car right now, or we will call the police." I was ashamed of my actions thus far, but I explained they were for a noble cause. I told Douglas that I was trying to get a copy of *USA Today* because it was a special Back to the Future Day edition. As I was trying to calm him down and further detail the reasoning for my actions, I pulled out my cell phone and showed him the Instagram post. As he studied it, his fiery demeanor quickly became more understanding. Douglas asked me to follow him up to the front, and he grabbed a copy off the main table in the foyer of the hotel. Douglas handed it to me and sent me on my way. As I walked back to my not-technically-legally-parked truck, I glanced down at my watch again; it read 10:01. *Damn, I'm late!*

That was the beginning of a day filled with all types of *Back to the Future*-related activities. I was in a group chat with my podcast co-hosts, and we were all gleeful with Future joy, keeping each other in the loop about the goings-on of the historic day. One co-host went to an all-day showing of the trilogy at a local movie theater, and the other followed in my footsteps to track down his own copies of *USA Today*. Needless to say, *Back to the Future* fever was in the air, and not just for the die-hard fans.

Allow us to look back on an exquisite day in the past. The most joyous of occasions, equitable to the day a young man gets his first kiss, a ten-year-old gets to ride Pirates of the Caribbean during her first trip to Disneyland, or perhaps even your wedding day. Several key events happened on that fateful day in October, but the one group of people who went above and beyond to show their appreciation for the world created by the Bobs were the citizens of Reston, Virginia. On that day in 2015, they became the citizens of Hill Valley, Virginia. Yes, you read that right.

The city of Reston changed its name legally to Hill Valley to commemorate Future Day. Reston is home to the Washington West Film Festival, a festival that blends the worlds of film and philanthropy. The festival was founded in 2011 with the idea that a top-notch film festival could bring some of the best new films to Reston and inspire change in communities. The founder of the festival, Brad Russell, set out to do this by donating all the box office funds for the five-day festival to communities in need. In 2015, Brad Russell had a celebration by hosting the fifth festival that began coincidentally on October 21. Earlier in the year, the Fairfax County Board of Supervisors passed a resolution allowing Reston, Virginia, to symbolically change the city's name to Hill Valley during the five days of the Washington West Film Festival.

Over the five days, Hill Valley, Virginia, hosted two *Back to the Future*-related events to bookend the film festival. On Future Day proper, the festival showed a *Back to the Future* trilogy marathon. On October 25, there was a red-carpet screening of *Back to the Future*, which had some special guests, including Christopher Lloyd, Bob Gale, and Claudia Wells. To top it off, all the proceeds from the event benefited the Michael J. Fox Foundation for Parkinson's Research. Brad Russell, speaking of the occasion to Reston, said, "*Back to the Future* represents for us the idea of dreaming what could be and the potential personal impact every individual can have on the future. Washington West is entirely about inspiring innovative ways to change our future and our world." Reston wasn't the only town in 2015 to change its name to Hill Valley.

Although it wasn't on Future Day, the city of Augusta, Kansas, changed its name for twenty-four hours to Hill Valley in July to celebrate the thirtieth anniversary of the release of the first film. The city didn't just change its name—it hosted a marathon as well as a Marty McFly look-alike contest, a citywide parade, and a cookout.

Another highlight of Future Day was the release of an item from the second film. Most people remember Marty walking into Lou's Cafe in 1955 and ordering a Pepsi Free, but everyone remembers when Marty walked into the Café 80s and ordered a Pepsi Perfect. PepsiCo announced on October 5, 2015, that they would be introducing Pepsi Perfect to the public on Future Day. When asked why Pepsi was creating the futuristic beverage, Lou Arbetter, the senior director of marketing at PepsiCo, responded by saying, "The *Back to the Future* trilogy was as big a moment in pop culture history then as it is now, thirty years later. We are excited to be part of this moment and to bring fans something only Pepsi could deliver—and there's no need to wait—the future is now!" The bottles of Pepsi Perfect were to be released at midnight on October 21 for $20.15. That seems steep, given the soda was first referred to as "Brad's Drink," but I guess inflation is as real as they say it is, and there's no breaks for another Brad.

PepsiCo and *Back to the Future* collectors alike were eagerly counting down the hours to midnight, but when they went to purchase the product (me included), many of us were disappointed to find out it went on sale a few hours earlier and sold out almost instantly. Six thousand five hundred lucky people purchased a bottle of the perfect soda, and the rest of us were none too pleased being left out of the fun. Pepsi knew there was an issue with the release and that they had fumbled the football, so to their credit, they announced almost immediately that they would release another 6,500 bottles to the public the following month. I am pleased to say I was one of the lucky few to score a bottle.

Back to the Future fans got several more treats on Future Day, including the debut of the first issue of IDW's *Back to the Future: Untold Tales and Alternate Timelines* comic series, which was the brainchild of Bob Gale, the *Back in Time* documentary, the *OUTATIME* documentary world premiere, and an incredible rerelease of the *Back to the Future* trilogy on Blu-ray and DVD, including a new short movie *Doc Brown Saves the World* and *Back to the Future: The Animated Series* on DVD.

This DVD and Blu-Ray set in 2015 cost about eighty-eight dollars and was worth every penny. The collector's set came encased in a working flux capacitor with a bonus disc celebrating Future Day. The "2015 Message from Doc Brown" begins with a scene in a smoky all-white laboratory, with the background illuminated by the lights of unidentified lab equipment. To the right of the screen, we see a whiteboard with a timeline drawn from one side to the other and labeled "space-time continuum." The board displayed six different time periods that were traveled to in the films: 1885, 1955, 1985A, 1985B, 1985C, and 2015, with arrows showing the order in which the years were visited by Doc and Marty. In the front of the frame is the blue glow of the DeLorean time machine, and as the camera pans, we see the inventor of time travel, Doc Brown.

Doc says that if his calculations are correct, the day is October 21, 2015, and the future isn't quite what we thought. The message from Doc led to the short film featured on the bonus disc of the collector's set. In *Doc Brown Saves the World*, we see Doc step out of the DeLorean into the lab, and this time we can see more Easter eggs from the original trilogy. Next to the unidentified lab equipment we saw in Doc's message, we see two podiums displaying the Nike Air

MAGs (announced on Future Day and auctioned off for Michael J. Fox's charity) and the Black and Decker food hydrator, both featured in *Back to the Future Part II*'s 2015. Doc looks into the camera and introduces himself as the CEO, CFO, COO, and CTO of Doc Brown Enterprises, Incorporated. Doc recaps what he and Marty set out to do in *Back to the Future Part II* and explains that the artifacts in the lab were those he collected from his trips through time, and he must attempt a major space-time correction. Doc tells us that in 2045, these items will cause the future to be a "post-apocalyptic hellscape."

Doc then goes over to the whiteboard and shows us the timeline of events from the films, then flips the board over to show the year 2045 and a major plume of smoke from an apparent nuclear fallout (side note: remember to get one of those radiation suits Doc had just to be safe) and explains that the artifacts must be destroyed to prevent this catastrophic future. The food hydrator apparently causes mass obesity because if you hydrate food that had been previously hydrated, you could double the food. The self-lacing shoes render all other footwear obsolete (except for slippers) due to the inability of people to bend over to tie their shoes. The hoverboard leads to the hovercar, and in 2021 there was a massive trash buildup from people throwing trash out of their hovercars onto the ground below. To combat this, millions of people buy the Mr. Fusion to dispose of the trash, and over one hundred million units are produced. Each Mr. Fusion has a small nuclear reactor in it, and on October 21, 2045, all one hundred million units explode simultaneously, causing quite the boom.

In this video, being produced for Marty McFly in case Doc is unsuccessful in his mission to destroy these items and save the planet, Doc tells Marty the cause of all these events leading up to 2045. Doc goes back into the DeLorean and retrieves a futuristic tablet that shows a headline from the *Hill Valley Telegraph* that reads that Griff

Tannen (grandson of Biff Tannen) founded GriffTech. Apparently, after Marty foiled Griff's plot in 2015 and sent Griff and his gang into the courthouse, Griff vowed to get back at everyone who laughed at him that day. Griff invents a social network that allows inanimate objects to post selfies, and kids love the app. However, it is revealed to be a scam that allows GriffTech to gain access to every object on Earth. On the thirtieth anniversary of Griff's arrest, Griff uploads a virus via his social network that is supposed to say "butthead" on everything, but a short circuit causes all the Mr. Fusions to explode. Doc leaves in the time machine to go save the world, and we see all the items erased from existence in the frame as Doc returns claiming success. The *Hill Valley Telegraph*'s headline changes on Doc's tablet from "Griff Tannen Founds GriffTech" to "Griff Tannen Found Guilty." We think everything is fine until Doc sees one item he forgot he picked up in 2075, and then another Doc shows up from an alternate timeline, and we are back where we started. This short was fun and a smart way to explain why certain inventions weren't in our current 2015.

Another surprise for Future fans came late in the day. Well, actually, this moment happened on late-night television. *Jimmy Kimmel Live!* had something as electric as a bolt of lightning in store for his studio and television audiences on that night's show. Jimmy began his monologue by acknowledging the significance of the day. Jimmy said that part of the fun of seeing the future in 2015 was to see "what life might be like thirty years in the future." Just as soon as he made that statement, the lights in the studio began to flicker. We then saw a series of flashing lights and heard a familiar Alan Silvestri score.

The camera panned over to the side stage where the DeLorean time machine made quite the spectacular entrance. As the car came more into focus, two figures in the driver and passenger seats became clear. Once the gull-wing doors of the time machine opened, Michael J. Fox and Christopher Lloyd emerged, draped in their familiar costumes from their time-altering saga. The two legendary actors did not appear as themselves but as their characters. The audience erupted to their feet; the standing ovation lasted so long that Marty checked his watch—great move, Mr. McFly.

As the applause began to wind down, Doc yelled out to the crowd his famous line, "Great Scott!" After Marty McFly asked Doc where they were, the great doctor confirmed that they indeed were in the future. When Marty asked if the audience drove to the studio in their flying cars, Kimmel interrupted the time travelers and said we never figured out flying cars and that they had disrupted his talk show. Doc inquired about the whereabouts of the King of Late Night, Johnny Carson, and then the biggest laugh of the skit came when Marty asked if they were on television. Jimmy said, "People are watching us on TV right now, although honestly, most people will probably watch us on their phone on the toilet tomorrow."

Jimmy explained there was no peace in the Middle East, no flying cars; there were hoverboards by name only, the Cubs were in the playoffs, and he filled Doc and Marty in on what smartphones are. Interrupting their banter, someone using a megaphone informed them they were "too darn loud," which of course was revealed to be Huey Lewis reprising his role from the first film. The segment came to a close as Doc went to repair the timeline and Kimmel asked him what happens in his future.

Although we did get a lot of great inventions that Robert Zemeckis and Bob Gale created, we didn't get everything we wanted. We got big screen televisions, video calls with Skype, and a *Jaws 19* trailer released by Universal Studios. But again, we never got the flying cars or automatically fitting clothing. Oddly enough, people don't have fax machines in their houses anymore (people don't use fax machines at all), but Bob and Bob saw October 21, 2015, before any of us ever could. Sure, the future is much different than it was depicted in *Back to the Future Part II*. But like the great Doc said, the future is what we make it. We have had a lot of human innovation over the three-plus decades since the second film, and we will continue to innovate and create. Given the invention of the Tesla CyberTruck, a flying car might not be out of the realm of possibility, but hopefully they don't look so boxy.

CHAPTER 8

IT'S LIKE IT'S BEEN ERASED:

THE CUT SCENES THAT MADE *BACK TO THE FUTURE* PEPSI PERFECT

Quentin Tarantino is not only one of the greatest living directors but also one of the greatest directors of all time. Since the release of *Reservoir Dogs* in 1992, Tarantino has been a creative force in filmmaking. Though occasionally criticized for some of his over-the-top and highly violent scenes, Quentin has always understood what it takes to craft a blockbuster.

There is no doubt that Tarantino is the ultimate cinephile. His love for cinema is so profound that, in 2022, he released a book titled *Cinema Speculation*. This book is a fascinating blend of film criticism, film theory, and autobiography—yet, at its core, it remains a pure love letter to the movies. In *Cinema Speculation*, Tarantino makes the bold claim that there are "very few perfect movies," naming the 1974 slasher *The Texas Chainsaw Massacre* as one of them. During a conversation with Jimmy Kimmel in 2022 to promote the book, Kimmel asked Tarantino what other films he considered to be perfect. Tarantino explained:

> Look, when you say perfect movies you're talking about any individual person's aesthetic, but even trying to account for all aesthetics...perfect movies kind of cross all aesthetics to one degree or another. It might not be your cup of tea, but there's nothing you can say to bring it down.

Tarantino then listed a few films he believes fall into that category:

> I think *Jaws* fits into that. I think *The Exorcist* fits into that. I think *Annie Hall* fits into that. Some people say *Young Frankenstein*. I could say *The Wild Bunch* fits into that. And that's not even a perfect movie. Its imperfections are part of its glory, so let me take *The Wild Bunch* out.

Tarantino highlighted his point, explaining that a perfect movie is "something that's so unassailable." And in his final pick, he enthusiastically added, "*Back to the Future* is a perfect movie!"

It's hard to imagine that a movie as perfect as *Back to the Future*—and, in my opinion, its two sequels, which are equally perfect—could have anything changed, altered, or erased. However, believe it or not, the film that Quentin Tarantino and I both agree is a perfect movie did have some scenes left on the cutting room floor. Everyone knows that several drafts of a script are inevitable, and story elements, character names, or plot details that appear in an original draft will likely change by the time you get to a production script. But even during production, directors and producers might make the call to erase scenes from the final cut, even after they've already been filmed.

We've come to think of deleted scenes as a common practice nowadays, and we assume this was always the case. But it wasn't until the advent of home video that fans of their favorite films got to see footage that they never knew existed. The practice of releasing deleted scenes to the public became more common in the late 1980s and early 1990s, with the rise of home video formats like VHS and LaserDisc. Studios began to recognize that adding extra content—such as deleted scenes, behind-the-scenes footage, or director's commentary—could increase the value of home video releases and appeal to collectors and film enthusiasts.

One of the earliest significant releases that included deleted scenes was the LaserDisc version of *The Abyss* (1989) by James Cameron, which featured an extended cut and previously unseen footage. As DVDs became popular in the late 1990s and into the 2000s, including deleted scenes as part of the "special features" became a major selling point for films, contributing to the standard we now see for home entertainment releases. This trend continued into the Blu-ray era and onto digital platforms, where studios regularly include alternate versions, outtakes, and more in their releases.

So, when *Back to the Future* hit the home video market, "To Be Continued..." was added to the end of the original film. Then, during the 2002 DVD release of the trilogy, we were finally treated to those scenes that had almost been erased from existence. Like many of you, I saw this additional *Back to the Future* footage and formed my opinions about whether these scenes should have been left in the movie or belonged on the cutting room floor, as they were.

I discussed these deleted scenes on *Back to the Future: The Podcast* in late 2015 with my co-host at the time, Norman Benford, and then again in 2023 when I revisited the scenes from the first movie with my friend Frank Janisch. I've selected five of the cut scenes and edited together our collected thoughts for your enjoyment and reflection. The descriptions for these scenes are from backtothefuture.fandom.com and there is more that we do not cover, all of which can be found online. But the question is would these scenes have made *Back to the Future* even better? Or did the omission of these scenes from *Part I* make it the classic film that we know it to be?

SCENE 1: PEANUT BRITTLE

George McFly buys an entire case of Sophie Mae peanut brittle from a neighbor, Howard, and his daughter.

NORMAN: Okay, our first scene is Marty talking to George in the McFly household and on the DVD cut, it's called "Peanut Brittle." In this scene, Marty is telling George that he needs to learn how to say no. Obviously, this is kind of important to the plot as it plays forward. Marty is literally begging his father to just try and say no to someone. Conveniently enough, after this conversation, a neighbor shows up with a kid selling peanut brittle for a school fundraiser, and he strong-arms George into buying the entire case. George doesn't say no—he surrenders his cash—and Marty just walks away in disgust. If I'm looking at this and deciding if it's a good or bad cut, I call it a bad cut. The scene is less than sixty seconds and it does a really good job of establishing how weak George is and how quickly he caves in. I think for the extra sixty seconds of runtime, it would've been better left in the film.

BRAD: Interesting. Now, I've seen the "Peanut Brittle" scene, and what's funny is that after the scene where Marty, George, and Biff kind of get into it and Biff lays out the groundwork for their roles, they cut to the dinner table. In that scene, Lorraine throws the cake on the table saying, "Well, your Uncle Joey didn't make parole again," and George is watching TV. If you actually look closely, George is eating peanut brittle. So, it's kind of funny that this scene was cut out, but the peanut brittle is still there, meaning maybe he just likes peanut brittle.

As far as deciding if it was a good or bad cut? I think it was a good cut. I do. I think Crispin Glover did a great job convincing us that George caved into everything just with his subservient behavior toward Biff. Lines like, "Alright, Biff, I'll finish these up and run them right over in the morning," showed us how weak George was. I think we already figured out his character without this extra scene. If the scene had been in the movie, would I have hated it? No, not at all. I don't hate the scene, but I don't think it was necessary—just an extra reinforcement of George's submission to others.

FRANK: Not needed. They demonstrate that in the movie when George says, "I'm just not very good at confrontation." It's all set up there. The scene with Biff and the light beer—it's all right there.

BRAD: Exactly, and where they cut this out, the next thing you see is George pouring peanut brittle into a bowl at the family table, with Marty staring at it, probably thinking, "Why is he eating all this peanut brittle?" So, in case you were ever wondering about that look Marty gives, now you know.

FRANK: And it's funny too because when you have that much peanut brittle—even without this deleted scene—it just adds to George's character. Yeah, George McFly would absolutely have an overabundance of peanut brittle for no good reason, because he's the complete opposite of Marty.

SCENE 2: PINCH ME

Marty McFly asks a woman on the streets in 1955 to pinch him, but she slaps him across the face instead.

NORMAN: Up next, we have the deleted scene titled *Pinch Me* on the DVD Extra. This is where Marty arrives in 1955 Hill Valley. He looks at the newspaper, realizes what date it is, and asks a middle-aged woman passing by to pinch him in case he's dreaming. Instead of pinching him, she slaps him across the face and moves on. Afterward, Marty hands the newspaper to a police officer, and the film progresses as it was released. I call this a good cut—it didn't move the plot forward or add anything significant. I just call this chafe.

BRAD: No, yeah, I definitely agree. There's no need to really go in-depth about this. I think it's a great cut actually. I don't think it's just a good cut; I think it's a *great* cut. Definitely not needed at all. I believe this was one of the scenes Eric Stoltz filmed. I recall seeing some footage of Stoltz doing something similar, or at least this moment where Marty figures out where he is. I think I saw this on one of the Blu-rays. But overall, great cut.

FRANK: It's a good cut because we know it's not a dream—that's all we need to know. It's more fun watching Marty slowly figure out whether this is a dream or not. Removing this scene actually enhances the film by elongating that process, letting us enjoy Marty's bewilderment for a bit longer.

SCENE 3: DOC'S PERSONAL BELONGINGS

1955. Dr. Emmett Brown looks at his personal belongings from 1985, which include a hairdryer, some cotton underwear, and a copy of Playboy.

NORMAN: Well, what we have next is a scene titled *Doc's Personal Belongings*, and it's where Doc is going through his suitcase that he himself packed from the future to travel to the future, but inevitably ended up in the past. He's going through the suitcase, and there's a hairdryer in there, some clothes, and even a Playboy magazine, which he hams it up with a bit. But really, the only thing of note in this scene is the hairdryer, which later shows up in Marty's Darth Vader scene with George. This scene kind of drags along, it's a little slow, and I'm calling this a good cut.

BRAD: Yeah, I've seen this before too. It was funny. I did find some humor in it, especially with the Playboy magazine—thought that was entertaining and kind of funny. But like you said, it wasn't really necessary. It felt like it was jokes for joke's sake, like, "Hey, can we get an extra laugh in here?" But the runtime of the scene itself being ninety seconds is what really solidified it as, "Okay, yeah, we've got to cut this." It slows this part of the film down. So, I definitely think it's a good cut. I did think the scene was funny and entertaining, but it wasn't necessary for the plot.

FRANK: I think you could take the Playboy part out. If you left everything aside from the Playboy part, I think it could work. You're right, it probably does slow it down just a little bit. I think they wanted the pacing to be quicker at that point in the movie. I'm curious to see how it would play if inserted and then removed. But for the most part, I agree. Going back to the gag about synthetic underwear—it kind of plays into him going through his suitcase with the cotton underwear and all that.

BRAD: Yeah. The Playboy part didn't feel needed because I kind of like how Doc isn't infatuated with women at all until 1885. He's all about the science until—*boom*—he gets struck by lightning. (*Lightning, Marty, don't say that!*)

SCENE 4: SHE'S CHEATING

Before the scene where Marty and Doc see George being picked on due to the "Kick Me" prank, Marty peers through a classroom window and is shocked to see Lorraine Baines cheating on a test (after class, Lorraine tells her friends she got an F anyway).

NORMAN: Up next, we have a scene called *She's Cheating* where Doc and Marty arrive at the high school and go inside, only to see Lorraine cheating on a test. Ultimately, the scene folds into the existing one with George stumbling down the hall. This was a really bad scene. The only thing about it that was even moderately enjoyable—and that's not fair because it was very funny—was Doc stepping over the bike as he walks into the high school. But it was an empty scene. It didn't do anything to advance the plot, and this was a very, very good cut. More of an outtake than anything.

BRAD: Yeah, I mean, it's a good cut, but I think—well, I think it's a mild *okay*. It's an okay cut. I could really go either way on it. The only reason I'd say keep it is because it further ingrains in us that Lorraine was not the woman she said she was. In '85, she kind of presented herself as saying, "I never did that with a boy, never sat in a car with a boy." She never did any of that and was kind of the good girl Marty always thought. But in this, we see she smokes, drinks, cheats on a test, and she's boy-crazy. So, it kind of reinforces that she wasn't the strait-laced young woman Marty thought of his mother.

FRANK: Yeah, I think also we don't need to know she's this rule-breaker so early. We kind of get a little hint of that when she says, "And he can stay in my room." And then later, when she says, "I swiped it from the old lady's liquor cabinet," it's like, oh, I guess Lorraine was kind of a rebel, if you will. So yeah, I don't think you really needed this scene at all.

SCENE 5: "DARTH VADER FROM THE PLANET VULCAN"

The uncut footage showed Marty using the hair dryer like a handgun, telling George to take out Lorraine, then chloroforming George, prior to doing so saying, "Now close your eyes and think of me no more." Marty then sneaks out of the bedroom window and removes the hood of his radiation suit, walking on a tree branch, then jumping into Doc's car, which ends with Doc asking him how it worked out.

NORMAN: Yes. What we have up next is an extended cut of the *Darth Vader* scene where Marty visits George and places the Walkman headphones on his head to try and convince him to ask Lorraine out to the dance on Saturday. The scene in the movie as it exists is a very good scene, but the extended version, which was deleted, was a very good cut because it's over three minutes long and, oh my goodness, does it drag on.

FRANK: I think it's too long, and *more is less.* You're going to hear George basically retell that conversation later, so it's kind of double-dipping. I can definitely see why they cut that for sure.

BRAD: Yeah, and you know what? Seeing him chloroform George is a little weird.

FRANK: Yeah, it's not just a little weird—it is weird. There's enough strange stuff in here to begin with; you don't need to be chloroforming your dad.

BRAD: We talked about how this is a perfect movie, but after seeing the extended *Darth Vader from the Planet Vulcan* part, I understand why the filmmakers thought they needed it at the time they shot it. I get how it even gives George the inspiration to write his novel—*Oh look, George, your first novel.*

FRANK: Well, it plays into that *Mystery Science Theater* feel, which is why this scene is funny. George would totally buy it because he loves that show, so that's why it works and is so impactful on him.

BRAD: You're right. I guess seeing it, you know what it was—seeing this long-form version of it showed me really how silly of a concept it is. Here's the thing: if I were to pitch the screenplay to you, and you're the producer, and you ask, *Okay, well, how do they convince George?* And I say, *Oh, we're going to put Marty in the radiation suit. George is going to think Marty is an alien because he plays him a Van Halen tape and says he's Darth Vader from the Planet Vulcan. That'll change his mind.* It almost sounds like, *Wait, you're going to do what? Pretend you're an* *alien?* Obviously, it works in the movie. Had they done the long version of it, though, I don't think it would've played as well.

FRANK: And I think when George goes to talk to Marty in the next scene, he tells him basically what we didn't see. So that's why you can cut parts of it and make the shorter version like in the movie.

BRAD: And George does say he "overslept" when Marty remarks that he wasn't at school that day.

FRANK: Yeah, he overslept because of the chloroform, but you could also chalk it up to him getting woken up in the middle of the night and oversleeping because he was *freaked out!*

Each scene was a lot of fun to watch and even more fun to consider how they might have fit into the overall story. As I mentioned, there are several other deleted scenes from *Back to the Future* that we haven't yet covered—like the Sir Walter Randolph cigarettes commercial, Doc Brown's quick conversation with the Hill Valley policeman (where he slips the officer a fifty-dollar bill which acts as Doc's "permit"), and of course, Marty's illogical fears about making advances toward his mom and what that could mean for him in the future. When you think about each scene in the context of the film, they were great cuts, and there's a reason they ended up on the cutting room floor. They helped make this movie "perfect."

And speaking of perfection, one of the long-standing debates within the *Back to the Future* community revolves around Marty McFly's character arc in the first film. Some believe that Marty is a "perfect" character—that he remains unchanged from the beginning to the end of the movie. I've never subscribed to this notion. I've always believed that Marty does experience growth and change throughout the course of the film. By witnessing his father overcome the fear of rejection, Marty learns that he can do the same.

So, when I had the opportunity to speak with Bob Gale during a radio interview promoting *Back to the Future: DeLorean Time Machine—Doc Brown's Owner's Workshop Manual*, I knew I had to ask him directly: Was I correct in my belief, or were those claiming that Marty had no character progression right?

Bob Gale confirmed my interpretation of Marty's growth, explaining:

> What you say is absolutely accurate. Originally, we had the scene when Jennifer says near the beginning, "This audition tape is great, you have to send it to the record company." There was actually a deleted scene where Marty wakes up at the end in 1985, and he's got the envelope to send to the record company. Earlier, he throws it in the trash, but when he wakes up, he pulls it out of the trash, and he's going to mail it. You've got it exactly right—he's over his rejection.

Gale further elaborated on the character's development, adding:

> And when you watch all three movies together, we establish that Marty's a little bit of a hothead in the first movie. Of course, he learns to deal with that by the end of the third movie.

This was a validating moment for me. After years of debating Marty's arc with fans, hearing it directly from the man behind the film, Bob Gale, felt like a confirmation of my long-held view. Gale explained why the deleted scene didn't make it into the final cut:

> It just kind of slowed down the pace of the movie when it was all put together. But that was always something that Bob Zemeckis and I had in mind. We shot it; it was all there. In fact, when you watch *Part I* again and see Marty coming out of his bedroom, he's got this manila envelope in his hand that he puts down. That's the audition tape that he's going to send to the record company.

So, while some may still argue that Marty's character remains static, it's clear from the filmmakers that Marty does evolve throughout the first film, and even more so over the course of the trilogy. His fear of rejection, something that hinders him early on, is something he learns to overcome, in part by witnessing his father's transformation. Marty also conquers his hot-headedness when someone calls him "chicken." By the time we reach the end of the third movie, Marty is not the same person he was when the story began.

When fans saw *Back to the Future* on the big screen in July of 1985, it wasn't the version that was originally drafted or the full version of what was shot. It was the version it was always meant to be—a version that has allowed the film to continually appeal to new fans, making it timeless. However, there was one scene from *Back to the Future Part II* that sparked conversation among my fellow fans, and it deserves a closer look.

CHAPTER 9

AMERICAN TIME STORY: OLD MAN BIFF

As seen with recent films like *Joker* and *Joker: Folie à Deux*, the *Suicide Squad* films, or *The Penguin* HBO series, modern audiences are as captivated by cinematic villains as they are by the heroes. Just ask any *Star Wars* fan, and they'll tell you that Darth Vader is as beloved, if not more so, than Luke Skywalker. This is precisely how I feel about the tormentor of Hill Valley, Biff Tannen. In my opinion, Biff is one of the greatest villains in movie history, and there are two key reasons why his presence on screen was as commanding as Darth Vader or *Mean Girls'* high school tyrant Regina George.

The first reason is the brilliant writing of the character by Bob Gale and Robert Zemeckis. Biff's memorable presence wouldn't have been the same if he were written any differently. His arrogance, brutishness, and relentless bullying were precisely crafted to serve as the perfect antagonist to Marty McFly. Biff's lines are now iconic, filled with insults and comebacks that helped solidify his place as a cinematic villain for the ages, even though they never made much sense. But whatever, butthead!

However, the primary reason why Biff Tannen remains so unforgettable is the commanding performance of Thomas F. Wilson. His portrayal brought Biff to life in a way that went beyond the script.

Wilson perfectly embodied the raw, intimidating energy of a bully, and his physicality and expressions gave Biff a menacing presence that made audiences both despise and remember him. Wilson's ability to channel the cocky, larger-than-life personality of Biff while adding subtle comedic undertones is a testament to his talent.

Before landing the role of Biff, Wilson had made a name for himself as a stand-up comedian and improv performer. He performed at legendary comedy clubs like Catch a Rising Star in New York, which saw the rise of comedians like Jerry Seinfeld, and The Comedy Store in Los Angeles, where he shared stages with Robin Williams, Richard Pryor, Billy Crystal, and Jim Carrey. Wilson's comedic roots certainly influenced his portrayal of Biff, giving the character a unique blend of humor and menace that made him more than just a stereotypical bully.

When Wilson was cast as Biff, initially alongside Eric Stoltz as Marty McFly, he worked to perfect the character's physicality and bravado. But when Michael J. Fox replaced Stoltz, Wilson's performance adapted seamlessly. His chemistry with Fox was electric, and their dynamic became central to the film's tension and humor. As the *Back to the Future* sequels came along, Wilson further showcased his range by adjusting his portrayal for each version of Biff across different timelines and realities. Whether playing the teenage bully, the corrupt and wealthy version of Biff in 1985A, or the bumbling old man in the future, Wilson's performance evolved with each iteration, making Biff an even more layered and engaging character.

In addition to his work on *Back to the Future*, Wilson continued to build a successful and diverse career. While he's forever linked to Biff Tannen, he expanded his repertoire. One of Wilson's most significant contributions to the arts has been his dedication to his craft beyond just the silver screen. He transitioned into voice acting, painting, and writing, becoming a renaissance man in the entertainment industry. His one-man shows and personal reflections on the challenges of being typecast demonstrate his insight and wit as a performer. Even though fans may forever know him as the towering figure who terrorized Marty McFly, Wilson's career showcases his remarkable versatility and creativity.

In the pantheon of movie villains, few are as simultaneously terrifying and beloved as Biff Tannen. Thanks to the writing of Gale and Zemeckis and the indelible performance of Thomas F. Wilson, Biff's legacy lives on—proof that even bullies can become iconic.

Wilson's ability to tailor his portrayal of Biff has always amazed me. If you're not aware of just how many different versions of Biff we see throughout the *Back to the Future* trilogy, let's count them together. At the beginning of the first film, Biff is introduced in the McFly household after wrecking the family car in a drunk driving accident. He comes off as the ultimate jerk—selfish and arrogant but not entirely evil. Next, Wilson plays a younger version of Biff in 1955, yet it's still the same character we know from 1985. After George McFly knocks Biff out cold in the parking lot of Hill Valley High during the Enchantment Under the Sea dance, we see yet another version of Biff: the now-subservient errand boy to George in the "improved" 1985 timeline. That's already three variations of the character in one film, and if it stopped there, Wilson's performance would still be impressive.

But Wilson's range as Biff continued to expand across *Back to the Future Part II* and *Part III*, bringing the total number of Biff variations (and related family members) to seven. In *Part II*, Wilson plays an old, grizzled Biff in 2015; Biff's grandson, Griff, whose behavior is a little off-kilter thanks to his binary implants; and perhaps the most sinister version of all, the greed-filled, murderous "Biff-Horrific" from the alternate 1985A timeline. Wilson then rounds out his performances by playing Buford "Mad Dog" Tannen, Biff's gunslinging great-grandfather, in *Back to the Future Part III*. Each version of Biff or a Tannen family member showcases Wilson's ability to mold his performance to fit the different personalities and circumstances, all while keeping the essence of the character intact.

During the second season of *Back to the Future: The Podcast*, Biff became a hotly debated subject. As discussed in the last chapter, on the podcast we did a "Good Cut/Bad Cut" series of episodes where we reviewed deleted scenes from each of the three films and discussed whether the filmmakers made a good decision cutting the scene or if it was a bad choice that altered the timeline in a negative way. We mostly focused on small scenes that didn't affect the overall story. To reiterate a few examples, there was the scene in the first film where George McFly is pressured into buying far more Sophie Mae peanut brittle from his neighbor Howard than any reasonable person could consume, simply because of his cowering nature. This was clearly a good cut. There was the scene, set in 1955, where Marty asks a woman to pinch him to confirm he's not dreaming, and instead she slaps him—again, a good cut. There's also a rather comical yet unnecessary scene where George is trapped in a payphone booth after calling the operator to ask for the time, and Mr. Strickland refuses to help him out (once more, a good cut).

For the most part, my co-hosts and I agreed that these scenes were wisely cut—they didn't add much to the story. But there was one scene that sparked a heated debate, making us question whether its removal was truly justified.

The scene in question was from the cutting room floor of *Back to the Future Part II*. For those who have never watched it online or on the

DVD extras, allow me to set the scene. After the 1985 Jennifer Parker is taken by the two female police officers to Hilldale, which was once a prominent area of town and now is "home of tranks, lobos, and zipheads" as one officer claimed, Marty and Doc go to rescue her from her future home and risk her running into her other self (you know, time paradox type things). While Marty is overlooking Hilldale, he sees what used to be the pinnacle of living in Hill Valley and fails to realize what it has become. Marty continues gazing upon his future residential area and even sees a dog walking itself with the help of some 2015 tech. Doc, after trying to help Jennifer get out of her future home that lacks doorknobs, frantically asks for Marty's assistance to aid the now-fainted Jennifer (who fainted after she ran into her other self; thankfully, no paradox occurred). Once Marty leaves the DeLorean unattended, we see Old Man Biff—the Biff who noticed Marty and Doc's time machine earlier in the day—get dropped off by a taxi. After the driver tells Biff to be careful because this is a rough neighborhood, Biff makes his way to the now driverless DeLorean. Biff then begins to go full-on *Grand Theft Auto* and takes over the controls of the DeLorean, sending himself somewhere in time.

Before Marty and Doc are aware of what occurred, Biff returns with the time machine. Something does not seem right with Hill Valley's evil elder statesman. Biff looks as if he just went twelve rounds with Tyson, and now an even more hunched-over old man exits the time machine. But not before he breaks his all-too-recognizable cane as he attempts to flee unnoticed.

Marty and Doc do not realize Biff was even in the car until much later in 1985A when they conclude that Old Biff gave Young Biff the all-knowing *Grays Sports Almanac*, making Biff the richest man in the world. But that's not our chief focus here. What we are looking at is the deleted portion of that scene. In the uncut version of the above-described "DeLorean-napping," we see a continuance of the suffering Biff was experiencing. Old Man Biff, again looking rather disheveled, crouches behind a car and looks at Doc telling Einstein to get into the time machine. Biff is attempting to remain unnoticed because if it were discovered at that moment that he had stolen the time machine, his plan to enrich himself in the past would have been potentially exposed, and Marty and Doc would have worked to remedy the situation right then and there. But, staying low and out of sight, Biff looks almost as if he is melting like the Wicked Witch of the West after Dorothy poured water over her. The old man is now breathing heavily, succumbing to more pain with every passing second.

Biff sees our favorite time-travelers fly off and begin to head back to 1985 without noticing a single thing. Once we hear the flux capacitor fluxing, and the time circuits reach their eighty-eight-mph requirement, the time machine vanishes into that dark Hilldale night. Almost immediately thereafter, Old Man Biff falls onto the dark, unforgiving pavement, just as Marty did when he saved George from being struck by a car. But this time, Lorraine wasn't there to nurse anyone back to health. Just as we see Biff slowly fall and hit the ground, his entire body and soul disappear.

You may have just read what was cut from the film and not think twice about it. You may be thinking that it was not a great scene and was probably best left on the cutting room floor. I know when I first saw the same scene, I did not understand it or care for it. But as I began to see why it was written in the script, I thought that it was a cut that could have been left in, and a co-host of the podcast said it was the worst cut of the entire trilogy.

If you recall, which I am sure you do, Doc points out to Marty that the picture Marty supplied (in hopes of proving that he was from the future) of him and his siblings was a mediocre photographic fakery because Marty's brother Dave's hair was cut off. This was the first clue that we as the audience were given that Marty should be concerned about more than getting back to the future. As the movie progresses, we learn that Marty interrupted his father and mother's first meeting, and he implicated himself in the event that led them to fall in love. Because of that, Marty has now put his and his siblings' future in jeopardy. Doc finally puts it together that Marty's actions have erased his future from existence. Doc warns Marty that he cannot encounter anyone else or leave Doc's laboratory until the night of the lightning storm for the risk of further damaging the space-time continuum and Marty's future. Even though Marty doesn't follow those instructions, he does his best to repair the damage he has already done. When we see Marty on stage during the Enchantment Under the Sea dance, we begin to see his hand disappear as he plays "Earth Angel" alongside Marvin Berry and the Starlighters. In what was one of the most frightening moments in the film, Marty eventually falls over, and we think his efforts to get George and Lorraine to fall in love were not enough. It's then that the two kiss and Marty is saved. But even though Marty's despair is only temporary, we all hoped our teenaged soon-to-be rock star did not ruin his life before it began.

The whole George/Lorraine/Calvin Klein storyline of the first film was more than just a fun way for the writers to spend more time in the 1950s. It also illustrated to the audience that time travel comes with high stakes that could result in events of the future never occurring or even worse—the loss of life. This brings us back to Biff. When Biff disappears in the deleted scene from *Back to the Future Part II*, we have to assume, given the rules of time travel in the film, that something occurred in the past that led to his ultimate demise. We know that Biff gave his younger self the almanac on November 12, 1955, and then he was still around and powerful as ever in 1985A, which many people who worked on the films and fans of the franchise refer to as the "Biff-Horrific" time period. That leaves us to surmise that something Biff did over the next thirty years caused him to perish—but what?

Also, another question that arises due to this scene is, if Biff changed the future by giving himself the almanac and was then erased from existence, why didn't that occur right when he handed over the book? Thankfully, we do have some answers for both of those questions. But before we get there, I wanted to share this with you all. Caseen Gaines, who wrote the excellent *We Don't Need Roads: The Making of the Back to the Future Trilogy*, came onto my podcast to discuss this topic and Caseen had a great answer to whether this was a good cut or a bad cut in the movie:

> **CASEEN:** Yeah, absolutely. I actually recall seeing it back in 1991. I don't know if any of you had the original VHS Trilogy box set that included *Secrets of the Back to the Future Trilogy*, a documentary hosted by Kirk Cameron. You can find it online, it's on YouTube if you didn't have the VHS set like I did. They showed that deleted scene, and it's funny how scenes get cut all the time. I'm sure many of you are familiar, or may be familiar, with *Little Shop of Horrors*, which had a different ending. They cut it due to audience reaction.
>
> In this case, there were concerns that the audience wouldn't understand what was going on. But I agree, it's a pivotal scene. It wasn't a scene that got cut for time. The cut actually added more ambiguity to the story, so I'm not sure how productive it really was.
>
> **BRAD:** I think that's where our conversation originally started—the scene in question. For me, when you see Biff disappear, it's

the final payoff we didn't get in the first movie. If you go back and change the past, it can drastically alter your future, even erasing you from existence. But I want to ask this: if they had kept that scene in, and let's say, for the first time, the audience sees Old Biff disappear in the future—which I believe happens in the first act of the movie—would that have tipped their hand too much? Seeing him disappear might have signaled to the audience that the payoff of being erased from existence was coming. It would've told us that something was seriously wrong in Biff's past, and by default, it's like knocking the eight-ball in; Marty and Doc win. Do you think that was their reasoning for cutting the scene?

CASEEN: It's an interesting question, but I don't think so. I don't think it would have had that impact. I only say that because Old Biff does return. It's not like he strolls out of the DeLorean whistling *Back in Time* or something. There's a foreboding sense to the moment when he comes back. Plus, the reveal happens quickly. Right after they return to the DeLorean, they go back to the alternate 1985, and the realization hits fast. Zemeckis and Gale practically beat you over the head with the fact that 1985 is different, even before the chalkboard scene.

There are so many signs: bars on the windows, Marty having to jump the fence to get into his house, and then the Black family living there when he enters. Everything's different. So, no, I don't think it would have tipped the hand too much. In fact, I think it might have raised more questions. I doubt the audience would've immediately thought, "Oh, something really bad happened." Instead, they would've wondered, "What happened in the past that made Old Biff come back and disappear? Is the past messed up? Is the future messed up?

> What's going on?" I think there was a missed opportunity to raise some intriguing questions that would've been answered later in the film.

Now, Caseen raises some great questions about this scene and does reference a reason Biff may have been erased. Indeed in the 1990 television special hosted by Kirk Cameron entitled *The Secrets of the Back to the Future Trilogy,* Cameron begins to discuss how we got the Biff-Horrific time period as a result of the almanac and then talks about what happened when Biff returns to the future. But, before I reveal Cameron's answer, which I am sure was a reason he did not just come up with on his own and at some point had to be approved by the Bobs, I would like the chance to float a couple of my theories out there as to what happened to Biff.

Imagine this: Biff goes to the farmlands of California to talk to the son of Mr. Peabody, Sherman Peabody, about attempting to fulfill his father's dream of breeding pine trees. While Biff is riding to the site of what will be the first fully operational pine breeding farm in the Greater Hill Valley area, his chauffeured limousine is involved in a head-on collision with a large truck that had the name D. Jones Manure Hauling painted in big white letters on the side. The impact sends Biff flying over the partition and through the front windshield of the long black limo. Biff is sent directly into the dreadfully foul-smelling back of the vehicle, which he was all too familiar with. When the police and paramedics arrive on the scene, no one else is seriously injured, but Biff is transported to Hill Valley General Hospital, where he eventually passes away due to the medical staff's inability to clear his airways from all the cow crap that has now filled his lungs.

Another possibility could be that Biff purchases a Ford Mustang (which Doc would never drive, ask Bob Gale why) or some other high-priced automobile. While driving recklessly one Saturday morning through the streets surrounding Biff Tannen's Pleasure Paradise, Biff hits a corner rather rapidly and kicks up some debris from the overly filthy streets, and it damages the hood of the car. To remedy the situation, Biff takes his now dented whip to Terry at the Western Auto store in downtown Hill Valley where he asks Terry to promptly repair his car. As he begins to make like a tree and get out of there, a mechanic rolls out from under a car and accidentally collides with Biff, causing him to stumble. As Biff tries to catch his balance, he falls into a large rack of car wax that begins to shake and eventually falls over on him, killing him on impact. When the police came to investigate the accident, they made a note that he could have survived one coat of wax falling on him, but two was just too much.

My final theory, before I reveal the actual explanation, is this. Conceivably, since Biff is so rich and so well-known by everyone in the United States and presumably the world, he may be asked to be involved in different forms of entertainment. I am not saying he's got leading-man potential, but perhaps there is a cameo here or a cameo there. During the late 2000s, Biff is called by World Wrestling Entertainment promoter and fellow billionaire Vince McMahon. Vince tells Biff that he has an idea for him at the upcoming year's WrestleMania pay-per-view. At the time on WWE television, Vince is playing up the *fact* that he is an evil billionaire and is throwing his weight and power around. Vince then tells Biff that he can come on the show as the hero of the story and attempt to stop Vince from doing any more harm. This leads to the two men embroiled in war, and Vince pitches an idea for a match with the title "The Battle of the Billionaires" for WrestleMania. Vince tells Biff that each man would select a representative to battle for them in the ring and even assigns a special guest referee to oversee the contest, WWE Hall of Famer "Stone Cold" Steve Austin. He adds a stipulation: the loser must shave his head. Biff agrees. As Biff and Vince see their two picks battle it out for bragging rights and follicle security, Steve Austin grows tired of the two men. After the match is over, the two billionaires are both given Austin's finishing maneuver, the "Stone Cold Stunner." While Vince is okay after the attack, Biff is stunned into lifelessness.

I must make a quick confession: the above-proposed way that Biff meets his ultimate demise is not entirely as original as the other two scenarios are. This idea is based upon a real-life wrestling storyline between Vince McMahon and then host of NBC's *The Apprentice* and future president of the United States, Donald Trump. Unlike Biff in my scenario, Trump was not injured at all at WrestleMania. However, the idea for Biff to take his place came from a 2015 *The Daily Beast* interview with Bob Gale. In the interview, Bob Gale reveals that Donald Trump was the inspiration for the alternate 1985 version of Biff Tannen. When I read that, I decided to replace Trump with Biff and spice up the finish of the match, brother.

Let's finally reveal the confirmed reason Biff was erased from existence in 2015. During the television special *The Secrets of the Back to the Future Trilogy*, Kirk Cameron says the following when explaining the cause and effect of time travel: "And just what happens to Biff when he returns to the future? Well, it's likely that his wife, Lorraine, shot him in the mid-1990s." There it is, folks, a bombshell straight from the mouth of Mike Seaver. Lorraine shot Biff, and that's why he disappeared. I tried to further research where this idea of Lorraine killing Biff came from, and I was tipped off by Stephen Clark from BacktotheFuture.com that Gale had confirmed this theory and it was listed on the website's "frequently asked questions." All questions asked on the website were answered directly by Gale and here's what he had to say verbatim:

> Our intention regarding Old Biff was that upon his return to 2015, he would be erased from existence because he had changed his entire destiny by giving his younger self the sports almanac. (Probably, Lorraine shot him sometime around 1996!)

Even though this is the official statement from the co-creator of the *Back to the Future* universe, there seems to be an alternate timeline of events that Gale has lent credence to. There have been a series of comics published about Biff Tannen, one of which discusses Rich Biff's death. In *Back to the Future: Biff to the Future 6*, the cover of the comic shows Biff Tannen being shot in the chest, and all you see is a gloved hand squeezing the cold steel of what looks to be a modern nine-mm handgun. The comic reveals Biff was killed by his great-grandfather Burford "Mad Dog" Tannen, whom we meet in *Back to the Future Part III* in 1885. The comic's timeline states that Doc Brown sends Biff to 1884, and that's the year Buford puts a bullet in Biff's back. Also, the same comic reveals that Lorraine shoots Biff in 1986 after Biff begins his bid for president of the United States but is unsuccessful due to Biff wearing a bulletproof vest. As comic logic can be, it's confusing, but I accept the fact that Lorraine does shoot Biff, as Cameron and Gale confirmed, as the explanation of why Biff is erased.

The reason Old Man Biff doesn't vanish the instant he hands the book off to his younger self can also easily be explained. Just as we learned from Marty's dilemma in the first film, altering the past alters the future. But it is not done instantaneously—it is done over time. This is evident by the picture slowly fading or in *Back to the Future Part III* when the tombstone erases one part at a time; it means reality has to catch up with events of the past, and it is not done as fast as it takes to jump through time periods. If it did in fact occur at the moment an event is altered, well, *Back to the Future* would not be an interesting movie.

This scene was ultimately cut from the film because it was confusing. In the same FAQ forum on the film's official site, Gale further explains:

> The vast majority of the audience did not understand it, so we decided to cut it out, leaving the answer ambiguous, and subject to various interpretations—besides the above explanation, you can believe that Old Biff had a heart attack from the shock of time travel, or from flying the car, or from something that happened to him in 1955.

I am not ignorant or arrogant enough to think I ultimately know better than Bob Gale or Robert Zemeckis and the rest of the team that helped bring these movies to life, and for all argument's sake, they are probably correct in leaving this scene out of the movie. But this scene in my opinion reiterated to the audience that the effects of time travel are real. Just because you could go back and change an event that you always wanted to change doesn't mean it will solve all your problems in the future. Although it seems cliché to say, everything does happen for a reason, and if you try to alter your density, I mean your destiny, there could be massive repercussions.

I truly feel that the scene should have been left in the film because it shows us that even though Biff would become the most powerful man in the world, not even the most powerful man in the world can avoid death. There is no amount of money, no amount of notoriety, and no amount of power that can prevent the one thing that every person must face. I think that having this scene in the film would've further illustrated that, even in an alternate timeline, the evil of Biff Tannen does not pay.

LETTERS FROM YOUR FRIENDS IN TIME: JEFFREY WEISSMAN

My Journey Playing George McFly

This story begins in 1983, when I worked on a film at the American Film Institute with a very compelling young actor named Crispin Glover. I told him I liked his work, and we exchanged numbers to stay in touch.

In 1985, I costarred in *Pale Rider* with Clint Eastwood, and I went to theaters to see what the summer competition was. Of course, I went to see *Back to the Future*. Already being a big Christopher Lloyd and Michael J. Fox fan, and having come close to working with Lea Thompson—I was cast in *All the Right Moves*, but the role was written out shortly before filming—I was excited to see it.

I was especially delighted to see Crispin's work as George McFly. I thought he was fantastic in his portrayal of the helpless nerd in desperate need of love. I called him and congratulated him on his great performance.

In 1988, I received a call from a look-alike agency asking if I knew who Crispin was and whether I was close to his height and weight. I explained that I thought he was taller and heavier than I was, but I still pushed to take a meeting as a potential photo double. I had read in the trades that *Paradox*—the working title for *Back to the Future Part II and III*—was in pre-production, and I could use the work to qualify my health insurance coverage for my coming baby's birth.

After a good meeting with the assistant directors, I was sent to casting, where I auditioned using the "hanging clothes in the backyard" scene from the first *Back to the Future* script. That went well, and next, I was sent to be fitted with molds to make prosthetic pieces, as well as to the production wig designer to be fitted for young George's hair for a screen test in the young 1955 George McFly makeup.

Meanwhile, I read in the trades that Crispin was not able to return to the role in the sequel due to conflicts with another film schedule. During my screen test with Robert Zemeckis and Dean Cundey, I was informed that Crispin would no longer be part of the production and that I would be taking on the role of George. Shortly after, I found myself on set, stepping in front of the rolling cameras.

I was sad that Glover wasn't able to reprise the role that he soared in, but on the other hand, I was delighted to be working and in the company of such immense talents.

We worked long, hard hours—sometimes up to twenty-six hours straight. We had to condense working hours to accommodate Michael J. Fox's schedule while he filmed the final season of *Family Ties*, which meant we had him nights and weekends. I asked Mike, "When do you sleep?" to which he replied, "In the limo between studios." We were all very tired a lot of the time, but we fed off each other's energy to get the needed work done and create a seamless story that picks up where *Part I* leaves off.

I have wonderful on-set and off-set memories with both cast and crew—stories that would fill a few chapters.

I was in New York to ride in the Macy's Thanksgiving Day Parade representing Universal Studios Hollywood when *Back to the Future Part II* came out. Along with my friends from Universal, we went to the movie theater for the first showing of the film. We cheered, for it was glorious to see my title card credit and enjoy the exhilarating final product that was so brilliantly crafted by Bob Z. and his wonderful crew and cast.

Years later, after *Back to the Future Part III* had been released, Crispin reached out to me. He shared his thoughts on the use of his life mask in the makeup design I wore and the way previously-filmed footage from *Part I* was edited alongside my performance in the 1955 scenes. I understood his concerns and reflected on my own experiences portraying iconic figures like Stanley Laurel, Charlie Chaplin, and Groucho Marx at Universal Studios Tours, where likeness rights were always secured.

During our conversation, I shared my experiences and insights, providing him with photos and details from my time on set.

I was not embraced by fans of the trilogy until the DeLorean Owners invited me to their conventions in the late 1990s. Then, I participated in the first *Back to the Future* cast and crew reunion at the Hollywood Show in 2008. It was great to reunite and celebrate the films with the fans. An unannounced appearance by Michael J. Fox on Sunday of the show stunned everyone. It was the first time many of us had seen the ravages of Parkinson's disease on Mike. He spent about a half hour with the six of us from the main cast, chatting and hugging. He was still his funny, feisty self, but the disease drove his body to move involuntarily at times, and watching him struggle was heartbreaking.

I have enjoyed supporting many fundraisers for The Michael J. Fox Foundation for Parkinson's Research. I produced a *Back to the Future*-themed cruise, bringing six of the cast and crew along, which proved very successful. The "We're Going Back", "Back to 1885", and "Return to Hill Valley" Parkinson's disease fundraisers were fan appreciation events that brought *Back to the Future* fans from around the world together—many of whom are known as "Citizens of Hill Valley," a close-knit group that lives for *Back to the Future.*

I especially enjoy the cosplayers, the fan art, and enjoy supporting the international groups in Argentina, France, Japan, Italy, Holland, Belgium, Poland, Spain, Canada, and Australia—all of whom have been united by the cause for a Parkinson's cure and a shared love for the trilogy.

Since the reunion in 2015 in London, Mike has continued attending fan conventions as his body allows. He is an inspiration and is deeply beloved.

I have been fortunate to experience *Back to the Future* as both a fan and a costar, traveling the globe, meeting fans, and making new friends. Even though the road wasn't always smooth, I cherish having played a part in making one of the greatest trilogies of all time—a story that continues to be rediscovered by new generations.

Your Friend in Time,
Jeffrey Weissman

CHAPTER 10

THE ALMANAC: FRIENDS IN TIME AND DOC'S DESIGNS

DOC'S DESIGNS

We all know about *Grays Sports Almanac*—the book that sparked Marty's lust for generational wealth, got into the hands of Old Man Biff, and almost destroyed the original timeline, leading to George McFly's death and Lorraine's bodily reconfiguration. Whew—take a breath, that's all in the past. When Marty purchased that book from the Blast from the Past antique store in 2015, it was akin to Eve taking a bite of the forbidden fruit. Needless to say, not a good call. I can't speak for anyone else, but without its introduction in *Back to the Future Part II*, I'm not completely sure I would even know what an almanac is.

An almanac is a reference book of useful and interesting facts relating to the world, as in sports or entertainment. Using that definition, I've decided to compile different lists and rankings from the world of *Back to the Future*. It's time we have an undisputed list (at least undisputed in my brain and heavily disputed in others) of the greatest inventions and, of course, the best versions of the time machine.

THE DESIGN OF THE TIME MACHINE

First, let's take the time machine. The DeLorean time machine is, without a shadow of a doubt, the greatest movie car of all time. When it first backed off of Doc's truck, you knew it was futuristic, scientific, badass, and most definitely would launch you through the space-time continuum. But, throughout the films, there have been several different designs and styles of the time machine. So, allow us to break them down and put them in the correct rank.

Number 5: The Western DeLorean

Many people I have talked to over the years have different opinions on *Back to the Future Part III*, but one thing we all agree on is that the DeLorean in 1885 is not the prettiest version of the car. When the car first lands in the Old West before Marty can even slide into 1955's slickest pair of cowboy boots, the car is struck by an arrow by a group of fleeing Native Americans that he did not expect, because he had begun thinking fourth dimensionally. Add that incident to the fact that the time machine had pieces of wood and electronics rigged together to create a quite unattractive hood ornament, and this version of the car is not off to a good start. Once Doc realized that the fuel line had been ripped due to the arrow attack, the two began pondering fixes for the unenviable problem they found themselves in. Doc and Marty pull the DeLorean through the uneven grounds of nineteenth-century California with the aid of literal horsepower. Then, they use strong alcohol to power the car, but it blows the fuel injection manifold. This just adds to the heap of abuse the DeLorean took in this film. Lastly, this car's somewhat awesome white-wall tires had been replaced with just rims to push it on the train tracks. Once Marty returns to the future, the car is destroyed. Without a doubt, this clunky hunk of junk might have held on just long enough for Marty to get back to the future, but it was not good enough to get any higher than last place on my list of DeLoreans.

Number 4: The Buried Time Machine

You might think I'm crazy for giving this ranking after my analysis of the 1885 time machine. But when I watched these movies for the first time as a kid, I didn't think anything was cooler than seeing the DeLorean inside the Delgado mine. When Doc told Marty to take a camera to document everything, I felt as though I was right there with them, watching them searching a mine for treasure. I love the adventure genre, and this was almost a crossover of *Back to the Future* and *Raiders of the Lost Ark*. I think that would be a more welcomed fourth installment than picking up with Mutt and aliens for that franchise, but I digress. As they approached a piece of the mine blocked by big rocks and pieces of wood with Dr. Brown's initials carved onto them, I could not wait to see what was behind the wall. Once they broke it down and revealed the time machine, it was one of the coolest shots from the entire trilogy. Seeing that DeLorean in a mine and untouched for seventy years, I felt as though I had just seen what was meant to be in King Solomon's Mines or Capone's Vault. The fact that no earthquake, no gold digger, or no other disruption bothered that vehicle for all those years made that version of the car both lucky and number four on my list.

Number 3: The Original DeLorean Time Machine

Typically, we believe that the original is the best. Think about it—New Coke versus Coca-Cola Classic, Rob Zombie's *Halloween* versus John

Carpenter's, *Fuller House* versus *Full House*. We widely accept the original as superior in these examples, but this is not the case for *Back to the Future*'s time machines. I mentioned when Doc first revealed the DeLorean, there was no cooler car. But after closely examining every iteration of the time machine for this list, the original DeLorean time machine is awesome, but not the most awesome! Sure, it's got all the things that you love: the flux capacitor, stainless steel design, the gull-wing doors, the big exhaust fins on the back, etc. But this classic cinematic vehicle does not have the feel that some of the other versions of the car have. It almost feels as though it was purchased off the lot and had some Adam West Batman fins circa 1960 added to the back. Trust me, I don't want to seem as though I don't love this car. If this was the only version we ever saw, it would be perfect. But in the same film, we see a superior DeLorean, which puts the first model, ironically, in the number three slot.

Number 2: The Time-Traveling Train Engine

This could be my most controversial pick by far, but the train time machine from the end of *Back to the Future Part III* looks incredible. So many questions come into viewers' minds when we first see the crossing arms come down on the train tracks in 1985 and a time machine train comes into frame. My first thought was, where the hell did Doc get that train? Did he commit another hijacking? Did his blacksmith shop really take off? How did he get a custom paint job as though he visited the now-defunct MTV show *Pimp My Ride* with Xzibit pulling up Doc's lapel and telling him that he had "officially been pimped"?

All of those unexplained events aside, that train looked awesome. Was Doc coming back at the end in a train a bit campy? Sure. That did not take away from the fact that if he was going to travel through time, he was going to do it with some style. The "ELB" initials on the side of the train, the staircase that folded out automatically, and the hover conversion that was revealed in the trilogy's final shot made this a sweet, sweet time machine and landed it at number two on my list, but number one in my heart.

Number 1: The Mr. Fusion Powered Flying DeLorean

After Marty gets a good look at his brand-new Statler Toyota Hilux truck and then sees his sight-for-sore-eyes girlfriend, Jennifer Parker, Marty sees a flash of light and Doc appears. Doc is dressed in a yellow raincoat, a red shirt with a transparent tie, and silver Bret "The Hitman" Hart-style shades and urges Marty that he has to come back with him to the future. This is when Marty, Jennifer, and we, the audience, see the best version of the time machine that ever graced the screen.

It's similar to the classic DeLorean look, but it has two new key features. First, Mr. Fusion now sits beautifully on the rear deck of the DeLorean where the plutonium chamber used to be, so this sucker no longer has any need to steal from the Libyan nationalists. The Mr. Fusion Home Energy Reactor is the power source for the time circuits and gives the vehicle the 1.21 gigawatts of power it needs to travel through the space-time continuum. Mr. Fusion is now powered with discarded waste from the McFly family's trash can.

The addition of Mr. Fusion gave the time machine a more sci-fi feel and made the car look that much more distinguished. The second addition to the car was the fact that it could fly! Is there a better end to a movie than when Doc says, "Roads...where we're going, we don't need roads," and then flies off? No, there's not, which is why this version of the time machine lands at number one.

DOC'S INVENTIONS

The next category is the top five inventions of Doctor Emmet L. Brown. We see Doc use many different gadgets to further his scientific and the film's cinematic needs, but we need to narrow down his best inventions. Not all of his inventions work, as we learned from the Doc himself when he exclaims to Marty in 1955 that he finally invented something that works, but the man has some great ideas. The fact that some do not work to the full extent of his imagination is a moot point. That does not mean they are any less great.

Number 5: The Brain Wave Analyzer

When Marty first arrived in 1955 after his initial encounters with Biff, George, and Lorraine, he sought help from the only man who could help: Doc. Upon his arrival at the Brown Mansion, Doc quickly whisked him into his home. When we get a look at Doc, he has a contraption on his head that resembles a miniature jungle gym you would find at Hill Valley Elementary School. Doc keeps the device on his head and then yells at Marty not to reveal the purpose of his visit. Doc proceeds to then stick a suction cup on Marty's forehead and begins to use the contraption to read Marty's thoughts. Doc asks if Marty had traveled from a great distance, which was correct as he had just traveled thirty years into the past. This spot-on guess led us to see the promise of this invention. But that is about where the success of the device ends. Doc then asks if Marty is selling subscriptions to the *Saturday Evening Post*, which was way off the mark. With that guess, this invention's promise left, but its iconic look lands it at number five.

Number 4: The Man's Best Friend Morning Café

One of the greatest opening scenes in cinematic history was also when we saw one of Doc's most useful inventions. I can hear the late-night infomercial now. "Are you tired of taking your entire morning to cook breakfast for you and your favorite furry friend? Save time with the future of kitchen technology, the only self-starting breakfast-making robot cook, the SelfChef 2000!"

In all seriousness, the reason we love Doc so much is because he takes simple problems and combats them with complex solutions. This Rube Goldberg machine is evidence of that. The opening scene shows us several parts of Doc's morning routine that start automatically, right on the tick of the clock. We first see the camera pan to reveal the first step of this process: an automatic coffee machine. Pretty mundane, but useful for a man trying to save time as long as he remembers to have a cup handy to catch the steaming hot liquid. Next, we transition to a timed clock whose only mission is to cause a lever to flick the switch on the television (this is where we see the news broadcast regarding the missing plutonium).

Another pan of the camera reveals burning toast, and then we see the robotic arm take a can of Kal Kan dog food to a can opener only to plop it into a dog bowl that already looks full and discards the can into the trash. A behind-the-scenes tidbit says this shot was famously done in one sweep of the camera. There was a slight issue that arose while prepping for this scene, though. The special effects department had been practicing with one brand of dog food and had to switch dog food brands at the last minute. Getting the dog food to fall out of the can properly was difficult, which one could assume was the reason for the single cut in the shot. To achieve this effect, the crew members had to heat up the dog food with a flame to get what they needed on film. That's something that I have always loved about the crew on any set. Just like Ian Malcolm in *Jurassic Park* once said about life, the crew will "find a way."

Number 3: The Western Refrigerator

When lightning struck the DeLorean at the end of *Back to the Future Part II* and we learned that Doc had been transported to the Old West, you began to wonder how Doc was adjusting to being a scientist living in a time where so much technology had yet to be invented. You would think that modern plumbing, the telephone, and other conveniences of the twentieth century would be what Doc would immediately begin to build for his personal use. Instead, the good old inventor did something else. He created a large, loud, noisy, and cumbersome machine that did not travel through time but took up significant floor space to do one thing—make a single ice cube at a time. This seems like a waste of time, but while you are shoeing horses and fixing wagons, a glass of iced tea does the body well. Doc inventing the icebox, solid choice for number three.

Number 2: The Time-Traveling Train Engine

You didn't think that I was done fawning over the train time machine, did you? The Time-Traveling Train Engine is perhaps Doc's most beautiful invention and his most impressive. I love this train so much because you have to think of the human ingenuity that it took to create it. In the films, it was never explained how Doc created the time machine in the 1800s. But if you jump online and read fan theories on various message boards, here's what we can piece together: we know that by the time Doc appears on the train tracks that pass over Eastwood Ravine, he has two sons, Jules and Verne. The oldest, Jules, couldn't be older than ten years old. You would then assume that as soon as Doc completed his time train, he would return to the present to let Marty know that everything was okay. So perhaps Doc had been working on fine-tuning this machine for over a decade. If you remember, Doc did not have ten years to spare when he was in fear of being shot in the back by Mad Dog Tannen. Like Tony Stark in a cave with a box of scraps, he made a flux capacitor, and the time circuits did their jobs. All of this makes the "Jules Verne Time Train" clock in at number two.

Number 1: The Flux Capacitor

This choice should not be up for much debate. Sure, I could have just said the time machine is the greatest invention coming from the constantly-in-crisis scientist, but no, the DeLorean time machine isn't number one. Without the flux capacitor, nothing else on the car matters. The flux capacitor is such an incredible invention because it is what makes time travel possible, and it took Doc almost three whole decades to finally create something that he first thought of on that November day back in 1955. I recently slipped in my bathroom, and my cranium grazed the side of the wall as I went down. As I got up, I felt this overwhelming sense of sadness and despair. I tried to find the source of my sadness and then it hit me like a bolt of lightning. I have not invented anything, let alone Doc's greatest invention, the flux capacitor.

THE ALMANAC: FRIENDS IN TIME

Throughout all of the adventures over the three films, Marty and Doc ran into many different characters who each had their own individualism that made them memorable. When thinking of the most memorable or interesting characters from the cinematic trilogy, I first had to implement the Jordan rule. For those unaware, when deciding who the greatest NBA player of all time is, you have to first make the rule that you cannot say Michael Jordan because it's too obvious. In these debates, you want to talk about names that perhaps don't get enough love. So, adhering to this rule, we are omitting George, Lorraine, Biff (including Griff and Mad Dog Tannen), Marty Jr., Marlene, Seamus, and Maggie McFly from this discussion of the best supporting or secondary characters in the films. After making that determination, this top-ten list was perhaps the most difficult to compile. So before I break down all of my picks, I thought I had to make a few honorable mentions.

First up, we must discuss Uncle "Jailbird" Joey Baines. We only got to see Uncle Joey when he was an infant and Marty told him, "You better get used to these bars, kid." Every other mention of his name was just that, but he felt like a fully fleshed-out character whose imprisonment was a component of the sad state the family was in at the beginning of *Back to the Future*.

Another honorable mention is Biff's gang: Match, Skinhead, and 3D. These three were at Biff's beck and call no matter what Hill Valley High's head harrier asked of them. Their blind allegiance is worth mentioning, and one of them ended up becoming the Phantom!

The penultimate honorary mention is the "save the clocktower" lady. I don't know where they found Elsa Raven, the actress who portrayed her on screen, but it was excellent casting. She made me feel strongly about that clocktower, and I still have a license plate frame on my car that immortalizes her memorable quote and shows my appreciation for the Hill Valley Preservation Society. With those out of the way, let's get to the best friends in time.

Number 10: Otis Peabody

When Doc meets Marty in the parking lot of the then Twin Pines Mall in the wee hours of Saturday, October 26, 1985, we see Doc begin to stroll down memory lane and give us a bit of Hill Valley history. While talking to Marty, Doc gets out of the time machine and says that he remembers when there was no mall and the dirt that they stood on now was farmland that belonged to Old Man Peabody, an ambitious agriculturalist who had an idea about breeding pine trees. Doc's eyes widen as he recalls the zaniness of Peabody's idea, which is ironic coming from a scientist who just proved that time travel is possible.

After Doc is shot and Marty goes back to 1955, the first thing he does is crash into a scarecrow and then into the Peabody barn. We see all the lights turn on in the little wooden house as an entire mid-century farm family empties out to investigate what they just heard in the middle of their slumber. That's when we first see the legend of Otis Peabody, as he states rather memorably that the DeLorean resembled an airplane without any wings. Mr. Peabody's son then refutes his father's claim and shows him the *Tales from Space* comic book, which has a cover featuring a spacecraft with the appearance of our favorite time machine. After Marty takes one small step for man out of the car, draped in his radiation suit, the family screams and slams the barn door. Marty finds himself shot at for the second time in a matter of minutes (fun fact: Marty is shot at five separate times in these three movies), and as he attempts to escape the ranch, he runs over one of two identical pine trees. Peabody fires another round, striking his mailbox, while calling Marty a "space bastard."

Will Hare, the actor cast to play the pine-breeder, did make another appearance in the Futureverse. In a deleted scene that was shot but never released, Otis is seen again. I spoke with Stephen Clark, the man who runs the film's official website, regarding what he knew of the scene. Stephen told me that he couldn't find a copy of the original script at that moment, but he recalled the scene involving Otis and a police officer searching around for the UFO that ran over his pine tree. While out on the prowl, Otis encounters 1985 Doc Brown. At this point in time, both Doc and Marty had two versions of themselves in 1955 while trying to recover the almanac from Biff. I am not sure why the scene was ultimately cut, because it seems like a fun interaction, but I trust in the Bobs' choices and I am sure it was done for the best.

Number 9: Dave and Linda McFly

Before anyone tweets me about it (@bradgilmore, by the way), I know I am squeezing in two different people into the number nine spot, but dammit, if Tarantino can say *Kill Bill Vol. 1* and *Kill Bill Vol. 2* are one movie to fit his ten-film limit, then I can do it for purposes of this list. We first see Dave and Linda at the McFly family dinner table when Lorraine slams the frozen cake of a bird leaving its cage with the frosted lettering reading "Welcome Home Uncle Joey." Linda is worried that she might never have a romantic relationship, which then prompts Lorraine's telling of how she met George and how they fell in love at what Linda called "the fish under the sea dance." Dave and his father are laughing at a rerun of the popular 1950s situational comedy, *The Honeymooners*, before Dave has to leave for work at

Burger King. Upon his exit, he kisses his mother and then his father on the head, telling the latter that it was time to "change that oil," which causes an odd bit of laughter from Crispin Glover's character and gives me the impression that, given the chance, Crispin would have been a great Joker.

Dave is played by Marc McClure, famous for his role as Jimmy Olsen in the Christopher Reeve *Superman* films. We see Dave at the end of *Back to the Future* wearing a suit to the office in what could only be assumed to be a better-paying job than his previous one. We only see Dave in the sequels at the end of *Back to the Future Part III*, but we were supposed to see Dave in the alternate 1985. There is a deleted scene where Marty runs into his eldest sibling in front of Biff's Pleasure Paradise. As Sammy Hagar's "I Can't Drive 55" begins to decrescendo, we see a man being thrown out of the building and rolling down the stairs as 3D from the Tannen crew tells him to "never come in here again." Sound familiar? The man is then revealed to be Dave, an obvious alcoholic, and Marty approaches him, inquiring what is going on with him and the town. Dave gives him vague answers and wanders off into the city of sin and despair.

Wendy Jo Sperber, Linda, did not appear in the first sequel either due to her availability. At the time she was pregnant, but she, like Marc, would appear at the end of *Back to the Future Part III*. Both Marc and Wendy went on to score several television and film roles after the time-traveling saga ended. Wendy Jo's life was tragically ended early due to a long and difficult fight with breast cancer. She is forever remembered as our favorite Irish family's wisecracking daughter and sister.

Number 8: Terry

Terry only has a couple of scenes throughout the entirety of the *Back to the Future* trilogy, yet we still remember him. Terry is Biff's mechanic who repairs his 1946 Ford Super De Luxe after plowing into the D. Jones manure truck after chasing down (unsuccessfully, mind you), Calvin Klein. When I said we only see Terry a couple of times, I wasn't lying. He is in two scenes during *Back to the Future Part II*. Terry is first seen in 2015 asking Marty to thumb a hundred dollars to save the clock tower, just as his 1985 counterpart did when Marty gave her a quarter (talk about inflation). While Marty is talking with Terry, the two of them see a holographic news bulletin proclaiming that the Chicago Cubs beat Miami in the World Series. When Terry tells Marty that he wishes he could go back in time and put some money on "the Cubbies," Marty gets the idea of buying the sports almanac which falls into Biff's hands (thanks for that one, Terry).

We then see Terry again arguing with Biff in 1955, while Old Man Biff, who had stolen the time machine, looks on. The two debate the cost of the repair job, and Biff throws some cans of oil into the back seat where Marty is hiding, waiting for the right time to steal back the almanac. Terry is portrayed by Charles Fleischer, who was the voice of Roger Rabbit in the 1988 film *Who Framed Roger Rabbit*, directed by Robert Zemeckis and starring Christopher Lloyd.

Number 7: Douglas J. Needles

Hill Valley apparently produced several generations of McFlys as well as several memorable bullies. Needles is a rival of Marty and is played by the greatest bass player in rock 'n' roll with the most memorable name, Flea. Flea's character is first seen during a video call with the forty-seven-year-old Marty McFly in 2015. Needles is trying to convince Marty to commit an illegal act involving their place of employment. Marty does not want to oblige until Needles refers to him as "chicken." After this, Marty's boss fires Marty on the spot. During the same time, we hear about an automobile accident Marty had as a teenager in which he collided with a Rolls Royce and broke his hand. We find out that this accident was due to a drag race he had with Needles the day Marty got back from 1885 in *Back to the Future Part III*. However, in this timeline, cooler heads prevail, Marty avoids any such accident, and the car nearly collides with Needles instead.

Number 6: Jennifer Parker

Jennifer Parker was the object of this young man's obsession when I first viewed an installment of the film series. Whether she was portrayed by the breathtakingly beautiful Claudia Wells or 1980s poster girl Elisabeth Shue, Jennifer Parker was indeed quite the catch for young Marty McFly. Jennifer is Marty's biggest cheerleader as she looks on when Marty auditions in front of Huey Lewis's character. Even though he's rejected, her support for Marty does not end. She later encourages him again, telling him that he needs to send in his demo to the record company. After she is picked up by her father soon thereafter, we don't see Jennifer until the end of the film. Elisabeth Shue had a bigger part in *Back to the Future Part II*, including recreating the ending from the first film and playing herself as a forty-seven-year-old in 2015, but still, she never had a lot to do in the movies. We see Doc and Marty lay her unconscious on her 1985A front porch and only see Jennifer again at the end of *Part III*. Despite not being a focus of any of the three films, both Claudia and Elisabeth did a great job making Jennifer seem like Marty's everything.

Number 5: Clara Clayton

Clara Clayton, in my opinion, is the strongest woman in the *Back to the Future* world. Of course, Lorraine had to battle off Biff in multiple timelines, but Clara seemed to be a woman who had it all figured out. We first hear of Clara when Marty and 1955 Doc Brown discover Emmett's gravesite in *Back to the Future Part III*. Doc's tombstone stated that it was erected in eternal memory by his beloved Clara. When Marty inquires, Doc isn't aware of any such person and refutes the idea Marty floats of falling in love at first sight. Then, the 1885 Hill Valley mayor, Mayor Hubert, tells Emmett he will help welcome a new teacher to Hill Valley, Miss Clara Clayton.

While attempting to figure out if they could push the DeLorean up to eighty-eight mph with the assistance of a locomotive, Doc and Marty see a woman whose horse and carriage is heading directly toward Shonash Ravine. Just as she is about to meet her maker, Doc and Marty save her. Marty later realizes that Ms. Clayton was the schoolteacher they named the ravine after in the future because she fell into it one hundred years ago. Marty said that every kid knew that story because they all had a teacher they would have liked to see fall into the ravine.

Clara was an admirer of science, and that is why she and Doc bonded. With her sweet innocence and strong-willed determination, Mary Steenburgen ended up being the perfect on-screen match for Christopher Lloyd. She held the unique distinction of being Lloyd's first on-screen kiss. Steenburgen said she only took the role due to her children's love of the first film, and yet she is a large part of what makes *Back to the Future Part III* so great. Thank you so much to the Steenburgen children for their part in this. Every time I see Mary on screen, no matter what character she's playing, she will always be Clara to me.

Number 4: Marvin Berry

The voice and namesake of Marvin Berry and the Starlighters, Marvin Berry, is a character no fan of *Back to the Future* will ever forget. The fictitious cousin of real-life "Johnny B. Goode" singer Chuck Berry, Marvin sang the unforgettable rendition of "Earth Angel" that scored Harry Waters Jr., the actor who played Marvin, a gold record from the Recording Industry Association of America. Marvin belted out the familiar ballad at the Enchantment Under the Sea dance, and his peanut-butter smooth vocals finally allowed George and Lorraine to kiss for the first time and fall in love on the dance floor. When I spoke to Harry on my podcast, he said his famous scene was the first one the filmmakers shot after recasting Michael J. Fox as the lead role. Waters said, "Everyone was excited, we had all these wonderful extras, we had a live band on stage." He continued, "This was 1985 and there was no CGI, so things had to be set up for these major shots that are flowing through a dance hall and [it would] take hours to set up." Waters then told me to pass the time, he and the band began singing songs and having a time. I think this is why so many people to this day think The Starlighters were a real band: because they felt like one and Marvin felt like a star on the rise.

Number 3: Mr. Strickland

"Slacker!" is a term perhaps as synonymous with the films as any. The sheriff of Hill Valley High School ruled with an iron fist and did not mind telling people exactly what he thought of them. James Tolkan's take on the character (who seemingly does not age from 1955 to 1985) was one of a man with nothing better to do than lay down the law in school and prevent any one of the attending students from becoming an aforementioned slacker. Strickland appears in the first and second films, but Tolkan is in all three due to his appearance as Marshall Strickland in *Back to the Future Part III*. I have often wondered if Strickland was the most forceful fictional school official of the 1980s. When I think about how he would fare against the likes of Principal Rooney from *Ferris Bueller's Day Off* or against *Saved by the Bell's* Principal Belding, I bet Strickland would have no problem taking these guys down in a one-on-two handicapped steel cage match at WrestleMania (Triple H, call me).

Number 2: Goldie Wilson

We just finished discussing the strongest principal of the 1980s, but what about the greatest mayor in the history of cinema? Look no further than Hill Valley's embodiment of the American Dream, Mayor Goldie Wilson. We first hear the great mayor's name from a campaign car driving around downtown Hill Valley and proclaiming that "progress" is his middle name. Later in 1955, we see a similar car campaigning for Mayor Red Thomas, whose middle name was apparently "progress" as well, so I assume it must have been a popular name in California over those three decades. Jokes aside, this was a bit the filmmakers put into the movie to show that even though thirty years had passed, the more things change, the more they stay the same.

Before I discuss Don Fullilove's Goldie Wilson character further, allow me to clear up some long-standing speculation from the fan community. As soon as I began reading everything written about these films, I uncovered a theory regarding the bum who we see in 1985 Hill

Valley sitting on a bench near the Essex Theater, who Marty refers to as Red. The theory is he was the same Red Thomas, the former mayor. I remember thinking it made perfect sense and, for a long time, I perpetuated this theory. However, it was cleared up by Bob Gale on a commentary for the *Back to the Future* DVD set where he stated that the two were not the same and the bum's name being Red was ad-libbed by Michael J. Fox.

Back to Goldie. In 1955, he was sweeping floors at Lou's Cafe when Marty planted the idea of Mr. Wilson's future political ambitions in his head. From then on, Goldie aimed to clean up the town. He started right then and there when Mr. Carruthers handed him a broom and said he could start his adventure by sweeping up the floor. Don's genius line reading of "maaayorrr..." made his short stint in the film one of the most memorable. Goldie's grandson appeared in 2015 for a commercial about hover conversion, and that was the extent of the exposure for the Wilson family. Mayor Goldie Wilson remains one of the most remembered "friends in time" and hopefully one day runs for president of the United States.

Number 1: Einstein

Einstein had to be number one on the list, as he is the world's first time traveler. Doc's dog, the consumer of copious counts of Kal Kan canine cuisine, was and is forever the better of the two pups in our inventor's life. Now, allow me to address the elephant in the room, Copernicus.

Sure, Copernicus was a great dog, but Copernicus was only ever in 1955 during these films. Just as Doc did, Einstein lived well beyond his years by traveling from 1985 to see 2015. The oldest dog in recorded human history was a dog named Bluey, an Australian Cattle Dog, who lived from June 7, 1910, until November 14, 1939. That means Bluey passed away at an incredible age of twenty-nine years and one hundred sixty days. If we assume that Einstein was fully grown by the age of one, Einstein saw at least thirty-one years from 1984–2015, twice the years his breed would typically see. So, that fact would give him the crown of the oldest dog in human history. Now, I know my science isn't exact but forgive the crudity of my theory. Einstein is a scene-stealer and forever Doc's best dog. Einstein is always number one on my list of friends in time, as he's the only other living being, aside from Doc and Marty, to successfully make multiple trips through time.

CHAPTER 11

THE FUTURE OF HILL VALLEY

After the animated series ended and Back to the Future: The Ride was no longer running, many fans of *Back to the Future* began to wonder: what's next for this beloved franchise? *Back to the Future* has become ingrained in pop culture, not just in America but across the world. The film remains so popular that countless other television shows, books, and films reference the saga, including the highest-grossing film of all time, *Avengers: Endgame.* This blockbuster offers its own version of a time-travel story that challenges the rules of the space-time continuum established by *Back to the Future.*

In *Endgame*, Robert Downey Jr.'s character, Tony Stark, delivers a rather grim statement: "If there is no logical, tangible way for me to safely execute the said time heist, I believe the most likely outcome would be our collective demise." After this, Ant-Man (played by Paul Rudd) tries to reassure him, saying, "Not if we strictly follow the rules of time travel. I mean, no talking to our past selves, no betting on sporting events..." Stark interrupts him and asks, "I'm going to stop you right there, Scott. Are you seriously telling me that your plan to save the universe is based on *Back to the Future*?" Ant-Man, also known as Scott Lang, responds, "No." Stark replies, "Good, you had me worried there, because that would be horseshit. That's not how quantum physics works." Later in the film, when Mark Ruffalo's Hulk explains the mechanics of time travel to Ant-Man, Hawkeye, and War Machine, Scott Lang asks in disbelief, "So *Back to the Future* is a load of bullshit?"

The joke in *Avengers: Endgame* sparked laughs from audiences worldwide, especially from none other than the "Father of the Future" himself, Mr. Bob Gale. During an interview I conducted with him in March 2021, while he was promoting *Back to the Future: DeLorean Time Machine—Doc Brown's Owner's Workshop Manual*, Bob shared his thoughts on that hilarious Endgame moment:

> I just loved it. I really did. When Robert Downey Jr. said, "Wait, you're coming up with a plan that's based on *Back to the Future*?" I fell out of my chair! I couldn't believe how outrageously great that was! And then I got an extra kick out of the fact that after Scott Lang says, "What, you mean *Back to the Future* bullshit?" What do they do in the movie? They go back into the old Avengers movies, the older Marvel Studios movies. Even after they said, "No, time travel doesn't work this way," it works *exactly* this way!

The mention of *Back to the Future* in *Endgame* proves that the film is anything but "bullshit." In fact, *Avengers: Endgame* wasn't the first film to reference *Back to the Future*. Movies like *Bill and Ted's Excellent Adventure, Ghost Rider, I Love You, Man, Knocked Up, The Pagemaster, Ready Player One*, and *Black Panther* have all either referenced or tipped their caps to the franchise. One film, *A Million Ways to Die in the West*, starring Charlize Theron and Seth MacFarlane, went as far as to feature Doc Brown himself. In the film, MacFarlane's character stumbles upon flashing lights coming from a barn, where he finds Doc Brown working on the DeLorean. When asked what he's doing, Doc says he's conducting a "weather experiment." These references in major motion pictures have certainly kept the *Back to the Future* brand alive and well, but they aren't enough to satisfy fans' appetite for more *Future* content.

Like the preshow film for Back to the Future: The Ride, when Telltale Games released Back to the Future: The Game, many fans were thrilled with the game's cutscenes and storyline, seeing it as a continuation of the original trilogy. The game, a series of episodic adventures, was first released in 2010 and re-released in 2015 to celebrate the thirtieth anniversary of the first film. Bob Gale served as an advisor on the game's narrative, which featured the return of Christopher Lloyd as Dr. Emmett L. Brown. Voicing Marty McFly was AJ Locascio, whose performance did justice to Michael J. Fox's original portrayal—surpassing even the excellent standard set by David Kaufman in the animated series.

Players of the game alter the timeline several times before seemingly repairing it by the game's conclusion. One devoted fan even took the game's footage and edited it into two feature-length films, appropriately titled *Back to the Future IV* and *Back to the Future V*, worth checking out on YouTube if you get a chance.

Despite this, Robert Zemeckis and Bob Gale have both stated that another *Back to the Future* film will be made "over their dead bodies." I will say I've come to a point where I am no longer opposed to the idea of another *Back to the Future* film or even a reboot so long as the Bobs are involved. For years, I battled anyone who suggested remaking the movie or restarting the franchise, but then I watched a movie critic on YouTube discuss this very topic. The critic argued that if a new *Back to the Future* film came out and he didn't like it, he never had to watch it again. But, if he did love it, then he'd have even more *Back to the Future* in his life. Great Scott, the man had a point!

One night, while browsing Amazon Fire TV for something to watch, I came across *Spider-Man: Homecoming* (2017). As I watched Robert Downey Jr.'s Iron Man mentor the young Peter Parker, played by Tom Holland, I saw a dynamic between the two that could work in a Hill Valley setting. Let's be honest—if you heard that Kevin Feige, president of Marvel Studios, was developing a *Back to the Future* reboot with Robert Zemeckis and Bob Gale, starring Downey as Doc Brown and Holland as Marty McFly, wouldn't you be a little excited? And what if you knew that Fox and Lloyd would be involved in the film in some capacity? I know I would be.

Now, before you think I've completely lost my mind, take a deep breath. There are no current plans to produce any new *Back to the Future* films.

Beyond the musical, *Back to the Future* continues to thrive with new merchandise. Stephen Clark, who runs the franchise's official website, frequently tweets (or Xs?) about cool gadgets and memorabilia available for purchase. Fans can buy everything from Biff Tannen's Pleasure Paradise playing cards and *Back to the Future*-themed license plate frames to coffee mugs with time circuits that switch "on" when filled with hot liquid—even a flux capacitor that doubles as a phone charger.

In addition to this book, several others have explored the *Back to the Future* franchise. I've already mentioned *We Don't Need Roads: The Making of the Back to the Future Trilogy* by Caseen Gaines, which was released on Future Day in 2015. There's also *Back to the Future: The Ultimate Visual History* by Michael Klastorin and Randal Atamaniuk, which is a must-have for any fan, and *Back to the Future Almanac* by Rob Klein and Jennifer Smith, which details all the collectibles from the films. Recent additions to the *Back to the Future* literary world include *William Shakespeare's Get Thee... Back to the Future!* by Ian Doescher, which retells the story in Elizabethan English, and *Back to the Future: Race Through Time* by Marc Sumerak, a children's book that allows readers to visit different time periods in Hill Valley using a wind-up DeLorean time machine. Michael Klastorin penned a book about the musical titled *Creating Back to the Future: The Musical.* All of these are projects that I have read and loved! You probably could tell by how much I reference them throughout this book.

Back to the Future continues to live on not just through merchandise and books but through its stars. Michael J. Fox, Christopher Lloyd, Lea Thompson, Thomas F. Wilson, Don Fullilove, Claudia Wells, Jeffrey Weissman, Harry Waters, Jr., and Bob Gale frequently tour the world and make appearances at popular comic conventions. Michael J. Fox has stated that *Back to the Future* fans are among his biggest supporters, often raising substantial funds for his foundation, which seeks a cure for Parkinson's Disease. Long lines to meet anyone associated with the *Back to the Future* franchise are always a testament to just how much these movies continue to resonate with people.

There must be a reason why someone born after the release of all three films—like me—feels so deeply connected to them. *Back to the Future* has always been and will always be a huge part of my life, and I believe the reason so many others share love for the franchise is because not only are these films timeless—they are also generational. Over the past several years, I've watched the trilogy at least a dozen times with my two nephews, both young, and with my father, who was a teenager himself in the 1950s. And let me share a secret: they all enjoyed the movies equally. The films connect with audiences of all ages because they adhere to traditional values—the same values Steven Spielberg praised when he first read the script: coming of age, family, and love. These are themes that stand the test of time, which is exactly why *Back to the Future* continues to do the same. In an interview with *Backtothefuture.com*, Michael J. Fox shared his thoughts on what made *Back to the Future* such a timeless hit:

> I think what made *Back to the Future* such an immense hit is that it was cross-generational. Just by the nature of the story, its appeal reached people who remembered the '50s and sparked the interest of a whole new generation in the period. It was also a very life-affirming story about relationships, as well as a "what if?" movie, which is another thing audiences love. It's hard to analyze, and maybe it's best left that way. It's like Mark Twain's analogy between comedy and a frog. If you dissect it, you might find out what makes it work, but it'll die in the process.

During an interview with *Variety*, Christopher Lloyd shared what *Back to the Future* has meant to him over the years:

> I've done my share of work, and nothing compares to the way *Back to the Future* is ingrained in people's minds. It's phenomenal. Every day practically—and certainly when I go to Comic-Cons—people come up and say, "You made my childhood." Another reference equal to that is how *Back to the Future* fills the gap in a lot of lives of young people, who have gone on to become doctors, scientists, and what have you. So, a lot of gratitude, and I feel really good about that. I feel very fortunate to be part of that.

Part of what makes *Back to the Future* so beloved is its perfect blend of humor, adventure, and heart. The film's playful take on time travel, filled with memorable moments and quotable lines, invites viewers to lose themselves in a world where the impossible becomes possible. And at its core, the story is deeply relatable. Themes of family, destiny, and self-discovery make Marty McFly's journey through time feel universal. Whether you're cheering for Marty to get his parents together, laughing at Doc Brown's eccentric antics, or holding your breath during the iconic clock tower scene, there's something deeply personal about the experience of watching *Back to the Future.*

But beyond the plot, it's the characters that have truly made these films enduring classics. Marty McFly and Doc Brown are more than just movie icons—they've become part of our collective consciousness. The friendship between these two, though unconventional, is filled with loyalty, love, and mutual respect. It's a bond that transcends time and space, much like the films themselves. Their chemistry and charm are a big part of why audiences return to *Back to the Future* time and time again. We feel connected to them, as though they're old friends we enjoy revisiting.

Who knows if we'll ever get more *Back to the Future* films. As much as fans (me included), dream of seeing Marty and Doc fire up the DeLorean once more, both Bob Gale and Robert Zemeckis have been adamant that the trilogy will remain untouched. Yet, as time passes and new generations discover the magic of Hill Valley, the hunger for more *Back to the Future* content never truly fades. For now, the musical, the IDW comic books, and the upcoming fortieth-anniversary celebration of the film seem to provide a satisfying way to keep the spirit of *Back to the Future* alive. These extensions of the franchise—whether it's hearing familiar tunes in a new context on stage or seeing the time-traveling adventures continue in comic form—help fans reconnect with the world they've loved for so long.

But the question lingers: Will we ever see more on the big screen? I don't think we can ever count it out entirely. After all, Hollywood has a way of reviving beloved properties when the time is right, and

Back to the Future's influence on pop culture is undeniable. As long as the creative geniuses of Bob Gale and Robert Zemeckis are with us, there's always a glimmer of hope that Hill Valley could one day expand beyond the confines of Universal Studios' backlot. Perhaps we'll see new stories, new faces, and new adventures set in the world of *Back to the Future*. Or maybe the saga will simply remain a perfectly preserved time capsule—a trilogy that stands untouched as a cinematic treasure. Either way, the future is wide open, and that's exactly what makes it so exciting.

But for now, we'll just have to wait and see what the future holds. It seems fitting to leave the rest of this page blank, because *Back to the Future*'s future hasn't been written yet, no one's has! Your future is whatever you make it, so make it a good one!

REFERENCES

ACKNOWLEDGMENTS AND SOURCES

The completion of this project would not have been possible without thorough and extensive research. I would like to acknowledge the following books, films, television shows, podcasts, articles, and websites, as they were instrumental in providing the information and inspiration necessary for the creation of this work. These sources have been invaluable in shaping the content presented here.

All quotes from actors, filmmakers, and other sources are cited within the text and are used strictly for documentary purposes under the Fair Use Doctrine. This work stands on the shoulders of those who have contributed to the *Back to the Future* legacy and the broader cultural context surrounding it!

BOOKS

- Gaines, Caseen. *We Don't Need Roads: The Making of the Back to the Future Trilogy.* Plume, 2015.
- Gale, Bob. *IDW Publishing—Back to the Future Comic Book Series.*
- Klastorin, Michael, et al. *Back to the Future: The Ultimate Visual History.* Harper Design, 2015.
- Klastorin, Michael, et al. *Creating Back to the Future: The Musical.* 2023.

FILMS, TV SHOWS, AND PODCASTS

- Aron, Jason, director. *Back in Time.* 2015.

- Ebert, Robert & Siskel, Gene. *Siskel & Ebert & the Movies*. 1984.
- Gale, Bob, creator. *Back to the Future: The Animated Series.*
- Gilmore, Brad. *Back to the Future: The Podcast* (2015–Present).
- Volk-Weiss, Brian, director. *The Movies That Made Us*. Season 1, episode 2.
- Zemeckis, Robert, director. *Back to the Future*. Universal Studios, 1985.
- Zemeckis, Robert, director. *Back to the Future Part II*. Universal Studios, 1989.
- Zemeckis, Robert, director. *Back to the Future Part III*. Universal Studios, 1990.

ONLINE ARTICLES, VIDEOS, AND INTERVIEWS

- Ayers, Mike. " 'Back to the Future': Why October 21, 2015, Is the Day Marty McFly Arrived in the Future." *The Wall Street Journal*, Dow Jones & Company, 22 Oct. 2015, blogs.wsj.com/speakeasy/2015/10/21/back-to-the-future-day-origins.
- "Back to the Future: The Ride." *Theme Park History* via YouTube, www.youtube.com/watch?v=N2b8Z1jxrio.
- "Christopher Lloyd & Tom Wilson Talk About Fearing Being Fired from *Back to the Future*," filmed at Rhode Island Comic Con by Dante Luna Media Group.
- Collins, Ben. " 'Back to the Future' Writer: Biff Tannen Is Based on Donald Trump." *The Daily Beast*, The Daily Beast Company, 21 Oct. 2015, www.thedailybeast.com/back-to-the-future-writer-biff-tannen-is-based-on-donald-trump.
- CollectBTTF.com by Eric Tate.
- Gale, Bob. "Back to the Future Co-Creator Bob Gale Explains How Marty and Doc Became Friends." *Mental Floss*, 19 Oct. 2010, www.mentalfloss.com/article/28526/back-future-co-creator-bob-gale-explains-how-marty-and-doc-became-friends.

- Hill, Dusty. "Dusty Hill Caused Trouble on 'Back to the Future III' Set." *Ultimate Classic Rock*, 24 July 2021, ultimateclassicrock.com/zz-top-back-to-the-future-iii.
- "Quentin Tarantino's Most Perfect Films of All Time." *Hypebeast*, 2022.
- "Rekindling the Romance: A Look Back at Romancing the Stone." Posted December 6, 2020, by Movie List. YouTube, 19 min., 48 sec. youtube.com/watch?v=XxPMCo07r7A%26amp;ab_channel=MovieList.
- "Back to the Future: The Musical—The Biggest Changes from the Movie." *XStreamed*, 27 July 2023, xstreamed.tv/back-to-the-future-the-musical-the-biggest-changes-from-the-movie.
- Gallagher, Brian. "Back to Back to the Future: Creating the Comic Book Featurette." MovieWeb, 25 June 2013, movieweb.com/back-to-back-to-the-future-creating-the-comic-book-featurette.
- *Later with Bob Costas*, season 5, episode 146, aired June 16, 1993, thetvdb.com/series/later-with-bob-costas/episodes/8592482.

WEBSITES

- "Back to the Future." *Futurepedia*, backtothefuture.fandom.com/wiki/Back_to_the_Future.
- "Back to the Future™ Trilogy." *Back to the Future Trilogy*, www.backtothefuture.com.
- "Back to the Future—Original Draft." *SciFiScripts*, www.scifiscripts.com/scripts/back_to_the_future_original_draft.html.

ACKNOWLEDGMENTS

Like everything in my life, this project wouldn't have been possible without the support of several incredible people. First and foremost, I must thank Robert Zemeckis and Bob Gale for creating the world of *Back to the Future*. If either of you ever reads this book, I want you to know that you have been my greatest inspiration. There has never been a film series that I've loved more than *Back to the Future*, and when the opportunity to write this book in celebration of it came my way, I couldn't resist. Your vision, creativity, and storytelling have shaped not only this book but countless imaginations around the globe.

Speaking of opportunity, I owe a massive thank you to the entire team at Mango Publishing. You took a chance on someone whose longest written work was a college essay and gave me the time, resources, and platform to bring this project to life. Your belief in me allowed this dream to become a reality, and for that, I thank you all. I hope this book lives up to the expectations and the magic that *Back to the Future* has given all of us; getting a chance to take another swing at this manuscript means the world to me.

To everyone at Mango Publishing, thank you for your support and your patience, and for helping me navigate the world of publishing with grace and enthusiasm. Your passion for this project mirrored my own, and together, we were able to create something truly special for fans of all generations.

Throughout the process of working on this book, I undertook extensive research and connected with some incredible authors and contributors from the *Back to the Future* universe. I want to extend my deepest thanks to a few standout *Back to the Future* authors, Caseen Gaines and Michael Klastorin, whose works were instrumental in my research. Additionally, a special shout-out goes to Stephen Clark from the great State of Alabama, the executive director of BacktotheFuture.com. Stephen's wealth of knowledge about *Back to the Future* is unparalleled, and he has tirelessly kept fans around the world informed and engaged. Not only did he appear as a guest on my podcast, but he also graciously answered several of my questions, ensuring that I got the details right for this book.

This book simply wouldn't exist without *Back to the Future: The Podcast*, which served as a launch pad for so many of the ideas that ultimately made it into these pages. I want to thank everyone who has been a guest on the show or worked alongside me throughout this journey. The list of contributors is vast, and I am deeply grateful to each one of them. This includes Robert Zemeckis, Leslie Zemeckis, Christopher Lloyd, Bob Gale, Lea Thompson, Don Fullilove, James Tolkan, Peter Rosenberg, Chris Jericho, Chris Van Vliet, Mikey Day, Eric Tate, Jeremiah Chechik, Joe Walser, Jennifer Trotoux, Darlene Vogel, Daniel J. Glenn, Kevin Smets, Jason from BTTF HQ, Norman Benford, David G. Mitchell, Crispin Glover, Claudia Wells, Jason Aron, Jeffrey Weissman, Kevin Pike, Caseen Gaines, Stephen Clark, Stephen Wynne, AJ Locascio, Harry Waters, Jr., Steve Concotelli, JJ Harrison, Ian Doescher, Booker T, Nick Jimenez, Scott Carelli from *Back to the Future Minute*, Jack from *Theme Park History*, Angela from Back to the Future the Musical Fans, and all future guests and contributors who continue to inspire me and make this project a reality.

And to my own Jennifer Parker—Farah—words cannot express how much your love and support mean to me. You have been my biggest cheerleader, standing by my side with unwavering patience and encouragement. Every time I doubted myself or felt overwhelmed, you were there, lifting me up and reminding me of the possibilities that lay before me. I couldn't have finished this book without you. You are my inspiration, my grounding force, and the one who makes everything in life brighter. From the quiet, late-night conversations to the laughter that fills our days, you have been the steady light guiding me through every page and every chapter. Thank you for believing in me when I struggled to believe in myself, for sharing in every triumph and setback, and for the countless sacrifices you've made so that I could follow my passion. You are my partner, my best friend, and the reason I dare to dream as big as I do. This book is as much yours as it is mine, a testament to the love that fills our life together.

I am incredibly fortunate to have so many supportive people in my life who encouraged me throughout this project. I owe my deepest thanks to my parents, Burrel and Marsha Gilmore, who have always believed in me and have been my rock through every endeavor. From the earliest moments of my childhood, they nurtured my curiosity, my love for storytelling, and my dreams of creating something meaningful. Their constant support and belief in me have been a source of strength through every challenge, every late night, and every step of this journey. Whether it was offering words of wisdom, being a listening ear, or simply providing a loving home to return to, their impact on my life has been immeasurable.

To say this book wouldn't have been possible without them is an understatement. They've been my guiding light, and their encouragement has given me the confidence to pursue this dream wholeheartedly. For every triumph and every challenge, they were there, rooting for me, just as they've always done. I owe so much of who I am to them.

To my grandparents, L.V. and Jerry Hughes, you have not only served as an inspiration—people to aspire to be like—but you also continue to be a profound force throughout this life of mine. I truly envision both of you on my shoulder in the times I need it most, advising me on my next move. And I'm happy to say, you have never steered me in the wrong direction. I love you both so much and miss you even more with each passing day. But I know that you're in heaven above, looking down on your grandson, getting a kick out of all the things I'm doing.

As I was writing the initial manuscript for *Why We Love Back to the Future,* I knew I could have done a little more, even though several extenuating circumstances played a role during that time. This isn't me being overly self-critical; it's me being self-aware. When the book hit the shelves in April of 2020, I remember coming across a review where a gentleman pointed out several grammatical mistakes or typos. Instead of being upset, I reached out to him and asked if he would help me re-edit the book. To my excitement, he accepted, and I was thrilled to have that opportunity for improvement. So, thank you Mr. Aaron Peck!

For this edition, I also wanted to secure a truly special set of forewords. I envisioned a dichotomy between someone directly involved in the *Back to the Future* films and someone who went on to great success after being inspired by them. The first person I contacted was Harry Waters Jr., who portrayed Marvin Berry in the movie. When I sent Harry an email, he graciously responded within an hour and agreed to participate. After a phone call, Harry finished his foreword just before boarding an international flight, and for that, I am a fan of his for all time.

Mikey Day was another person I had in mind for this project. A major *Back to the Future* fan, Mikey has been a guest on my podcast, and

I knew he would be perfect to represent the impact of the franchise on fans who then forged their own successful careers. I didn't have his email on hand, so I took a creative approach. I wrote him a letter, aged it by crumpling it and soaking it in tea, and at the top, I labeled it "Western Union." I put the letter in a leather envelope and sent it to 30 Rockefeller Plaza, home of *Saturday Night Live* and the inspiration behind *30 Rock*. Shortly after, I received an email from Mikey. He told me it was the coolest piece of mail he had ever received and happily agreed to write the foreword. For both Harry and Mikey's contributions, I am forever grateful.

I have to give a shout-out to my brothers, Rusty and Scott, and my sister, Brittney, whose unwavering support and encouragement have been invaluable throughout this journey. I also want to express my heartfelt thanks to my brother-in-law Gary for always having my back, and to my incredible nephews, Parker and Preston, who inspire me every day with their curiosity and energy.

I would be remiss if I didn't take a moment to express my gratitude to my incredible in-laws, each of whom has impacted my life in profound ways. Ayda, my mother-in-law, has always welcomed me with open arms and warmth, making me feel like part of the family from day one. Ihsan, my father-in-law, always offering invaluable advice and kindness at every turn. Amira, my other mother-in-law, has been a beacon of love and generosity, always there with a smile and an encouraging word. And Suad, my sister-in-law, but who feels like my flesh and blood sister in all the best ways, I love you tons.

A massive thank you to James Walker. He has always been supportive and opened doors for me and countless others. He is a true great and authentic human being.

Special thanks to Ken Napzok, whose success with *Why We Love Star Wars* not only fueled my own interest in writing this book but served as a guiding light in navigating the complexities of authorship. Your work inspired me to take on this challenge.

Additional thanks go to Aaron Peck, Phillip Schneider, Rodolfo Martinez, Norman Benford, and Eric Tate for their insightful feedback, countless hours of revision help, and constant motivation that pushed this book to be the best it could be. Without their thoughtful contributions and attention to detail, this project would not have reached its fullest potential.

To my friends in time contributors: Chris Van Vliet, Roxy Striar, Frank Janisch, Jeffrey Weissman, Tony Ruscoe, Eric Tate, Caseen Gaines, Norman Benford, and Jeff Smith. Thank you!

To Michael J. Fox, thank you not only for giving us one of the greatest characters in cinematic history—Marty McFly—but for your tireless dedication to finding a cure for Parkinson's Disease. My family, and countless others, owe you more than words can express for the hope, inspiration, and vital information you've provided through your efforts.

Christopher Lloyd, you are one of my all-time favorite actors, and your body of work has had an immeasurable impact on me. From your brilliant portrayal of Doc Brown in *Back to the Future* to your unforgettable roles in *Taxi*, *Who Framed Roger Rabbit*, and *The Addams Family*, you have brought such unique energy to every character you've played. Your talent has shaped so many of my favorite films and moments. Meeting both of you was like catching a perfectly thrown frisbee—*FAR OUT!* Thank you for the inspiration you've given me and so many others!

I want to extend my deepest gratitude to everyone who has supported me throughout my journey. From the early days of making music with my brothers in *Twenty Eleven*—Avery, Tré, Dallas, and Tyler—to my *Reality of Wrestling* family, you've all played a pivotal role in shaping the path I'm on today. Those days of performing on stage, collaborating, and chasing our shared dreams taught me the power of creativity and community. The lessons and friendships forged during that time will forever be a part of me, and for that, I'm truly thankful.

And to the *Schmoedown* community, where would I be without your energy, your camaraderie, and your support? You welcomed me with open arms, and the friendships and moments we've shared have been nothing short of extraordinary. Whether we were breaking down films, competing in matches, or just geeking out over the movies we love, you all have been an integral part of this journey.

To the Pinheads from *Back to the Future: The Podcast*, your unwavering passion for the franchise and your enthusiasm for the podcast have fueled my own excitement to dive deeper into this beloved world. Week after week, episode after episode, your dedication kept me going and made this entire journey so much more rewarding. You've not only been listeners—you've become friends and fellow travelers on this time-hopping adventure.

Without your support—whether you listened to an episode, shared a kind word, or simply followed along on this ride—none of this would have been possible. We may be drawn together by our shared love of *Back to the Future*, but it's the friendships and connections we've made that truly make this community special. From the bottom of my heart, thank you for being part of this adventure. Here's to many more journeys through time and space, and remember, as Doc Brown said, "Your future is whatever you make it, so make it a good one!"

ABOUT THE AUTHOR

Brad Gilmore is a writer, television host, and radio personality born and raised in Houston, Texas. Over the course of his career, Gilmore has lent his talents to several prestigious platforms, including **CW39** and **ESPN Radio**. As the creator and host of *The Collection*, Brad conducts insightful interviews with leading figures from the worlds of film, television, music, and sports. Additionally, he serves as the executive producer and host of *Back to the Future: The Podcast*, an in-depth exploration of the iconic film franchise, along with other podcasts, including *Clue the Movie Podcast* and more.

Brad is also the longest-tenured announcer for Two-Time WWE Hall of Famer Booker T's *Reality of Wrestling*, Texas's premier wrestling promotion, and co-hosts the critically acclaimed *The Hall of Fame* with Booker T. As a member of the **Critics' Choice Association**, Gilmore remains deeply connected to the film and television industries, frequently reviewing and discussing the latest releases.

Outside of broadcasting, Brad is an accomplished author, having published two bestselling books: *Back from the Future: A Celebration of the Greatest Time-Travel Story Ever Told* and *Bond, James Bond: Exploring the Shaken and Stirred History of Ian Fleming's 007*. Brad is also the founder of **Gilmore Media**, a content creation company where he develops screenplays, books, comic books, and projects for film and television.

Gilmore's creative endeavors extend beyond media and publishing. He is a founding member, MC, writer, and producer for the band Twenty Eleven. Brad also has a deep love for comic books and is currently working on several screenplays and comic book projects that expand his storytelling portfolio.

An alumnus of the University of Houston, where he graduated summa cum laude with a degree in communication studies, Brad also holds a master's degree from the University of Alabama.

Keep up with Brad and his upcoming projects at bradgilmore.net.

You can contact Brad at mgmt@cantwaitforever.com.

Mango Publishing, established in 2014, publishes an eclectic list of books by diverse authors—both new and established voices—on topics ranging from business, personal growth, women's empowerment, LGBTQ studies, health, and spirituality to history, popular culture, time management, decluttering, lifestyle, mental wellness, aging, and sustainable living. We were named 2019 *and* 2020's #1 fastest growing independent publisher by *Publishers Weekly*. Our success is driven by our main goal, which is to publish high-quality books that will entertain readers as well as make a positive difference in their lives.

Our readers are our most important resource; we value your input, suggestions, and ideas. We'd love to hear from you—after all, we are publishing books for you!

Please stay in touch with us and follow us at:

Facebook: Mango Publishing
Twitter: @MangoPublishing
Instagram: @MangoPublishing
LinkedIn: Mango Publishing
Pinterest: Mango Publishing
Newsletter: mangopublishinggroup.com/newsletter

Join us on Mango's journey to reinvent publishing, one book at a time.

www.ingramcontent.com/pod-product-compliance
Lightning Source LLC
Jackson TN
JSHW030303210425
R14054100001B/R140541PG82655JSX00001B/1

* 9 7 8 1 6 8 4 8 1 7 8 7 0 *